W9-BZX-480

THE
SmartMoney
GUIDE TO
REAL ESTATE
INVESTING

THE
SmartMoney
GUIDE TO
REAL ESTATE
INVESTING

GERRI WILLIS

WILEY

JOHN WILEY & SONS, INC.

Copyright © 2003 by SmartMoney. All rights reserved.

Published by John Wiley & Sons, Inc., Hoboken, New Jersey.
Published simultaneously in Canada.

SmartMoney is a joint publishing venture of Dow Jones & Company, Inc., and Hearst SM
Partnership, a subsidiary of The Hearst Corporation.

No part of this publication may be reproduced, stored in a retrieval system, or transmitted in
any form or by any means, electronic, mechanical, photocopying, recording, scanning, or
otherwise, except as permitted under Section 107 or 108 of the 1976 United States
Copyright Act, without either the prior written permission of the Publisher, or authorization
through payment of the appropriate per-copy fee to the Copyright Clearance Center, Inc.,
222 Rosewood Drive, Danvers, MA 01923, 978-750-8400, fax 978-750-4470, or on the
web at www.copyright.com. Requests to the Publisher for permission should be addressed to
the Permissions Department, John Wiley & Sons, Inc., 111 River Street, Hoboken, NJ
07030, 201-748-6011, fax 201-748-6008, e-mail: permcoordinator@wiley.com.

Limit of Liability/Disclaimer of Warranty: While the publisher and author have used their
best efforts in preparing this book, they make no representations or warranties with respect
to the accuracy or completeness of the contents of this book and specifically disclaim any
implied warranties of merchantability or fitness for a particular purpose. No warranty may
be created or extended by sales representatives or written sales materials. The advice and
strategies contained herein may not be suitable for your situation. You should consult with a
professional where appropriate. Neither the publisher nor author shall be liable for any loss
of profit or any other commercial damages, including but not limited to special, incidental,
consequential, or other damages.

For general information on our other products and services, or technical support, please
contact our Customer Care Department within the United States at 800-762-2974, outside
the United States at 317-572-3993 or fax 317-572-4002.

Wiley also publishes its books in a variety of electronic formats. Some content that appears
in print may not be available in electronic books.

For more information about Wiley products, visit our web site at www.wiley.com.

Library of Congress Cataloging-in-Publication Data:
Willis, Gerri.
    The SmartMoney guide to real estate investing / Gerri Willis.
        p.   cm.
    Includes index.
    ISBN 0-471-22399-9 (CLOTH : alk. paper)
    1. Real estate investment.   I. Title.
    HD1382.5 .W552 2003
    332.63'24—dc21   2002154134

Printed in the United States of America.

10   9   8   7   6   5   4   3   2   1

CONTENTS

FOREWORD

Many years ago, when I was a cub reporter on a newspaper covering business and investing, I had a big idea: I would hire a financial planner. I was making such a meager salary at the time, I figured a planner could help me make the most of every dollar I earned.

Since none of my friends had financial planners, I couldn't ask for references. So I called up the only investment adviser I knew—she wrote a weekly stock market column for the newspaper I worked on—and set up a meeting. I was thrilled. Just 23 years old, I was on my way toward becoming an investor.

But our session didn't go quite like I imagined. Sitting behind a huge maple desk in a dark-paneled office, my new adviser had just one question for me: "Do you own a home yet?"

"Well, no . . ." I explained. "That's one of the things I'm hoping to do with my money. . . ."

"Do it first," she said, cutting me off. "Save up all your money until you can buy a home. Only then should you worry about investing in the market or anyplace else."

It might be an overstatement to say this is the finest piece of advice I ever got, but it certainly ranks up there among the very best. Owning real estate has been an immensely rewarding experience for my family and me. From the first New York City apartment we bought in the early 1980s to the suburban dwelling we live in now, a stretch that has taken us through five different homes, we've had a wealth of great learning experiences, terrific tax breaks, and not insubstantial capital gains. We haven't yet bought any investment (i.e., rental) property, but I can assure you it's only a matter of time.

I am not one of those people who believes their homes will out-perform all other investments. Stocks, in particular, ought to do better over the long term. But our family home is easily my favorite invest-ment, and that counts for a lot. I love the way it looks, I love coming home to it every night, and I surely love the way its value has held up over the past few difficult years in the stock market.

Whether you're looking to buy a first home or you are an experi-enced homebuyer/seller, I am confident you'll find a great deal of helpful information in this new book by *SmartMoney*'s Gerri Willis. In writing it, Gerri combined her own firsthand knowledge of the real estate scene with great reporting and the incomparable resources of *SmartMoney* magazine and SmartMoney.com. I think you'll agree that the result is a practical but highly readable guide to a most important corner of the investing world.

Here's to home ownership!

PETER FINCH
Editor
SmartMoney

ACKNOWLEDGMENTS

Every issue of *SmartMoney* magazine has always been a collaborative effort. This book is no different. Over the years, a talented crew of *SmartMoney* writers and editors produced a steady stream of stories on topics that hit readers close to home—the purchase, finance, and renovation of their biggest single investment. My challenge was to extend that understanding into the world of real estate investment, whether that meant buying a vacation home, an apartment building, or shares in a real estate investment trust. *SmartMoney* Editor Peter Finch was instrumental in guiding my effort, providing the sharp and analytic eye that I've come to rely upon. My thanks to him for his patience.

Others, too, have provided assistance. *SmartMoney* Deputy Editor John Capouya has added his singular editorial voice to our real estate coverage. Managing Editor Nancy Smith has provided a constant stream of encouragement. Then there is the long list of *SmartMoney* writers and reporters whose efforts and insights were instrumental, among them Chris Taylor, Matthew Heimer, Chris Horymski, and Amy Gunderson. Special thanks, too, to Bill Bischoff, who guided me through the complex maze of real estate tax rules.

I'd like to acknowledge Steve Swartz and Stuart Emmrich, former president and editor of *SmartMoney*, respectively. Their commitment to the idea that individuals can take control of their financial futures has always been a personal inspiration.

Finally, I'd like to thank my husband, David, for his unwavering support.

GERRI WILLIS

THE CASE FOR REAL ESTATE

As a longtime personal finance journalist, I'm always uneasy when investing pros say that what they do is so maddeningly complex that individuals could never master it on their own. And that's exactly what I heard as I researched this book. Even well-known real estate investing advocates like Sam Zell said individuals should stick with real estate investment trusts (REITs)—stocks of companies that invest in real estate. But remember, the it's-way-too-hard-for-you-novices line of reasoning is exactly the argument Wall Street pros used when trying to convince us to keep buying their advice. As has become blindingly clear during the bear market, though, professionals aren't any better at managing money than the rest of us. *SmartMoney* magazine was started, in part, to explode the myth that individuals couldn't take control of their own financial futures. And that's what we hope to do all over again—this time in an entirely different investing arena, real estate.

Truth is, loads of individuals have already been doing quite well investing on their own (see Figure I.1). Most experts place the proportion of privately held rental properties at about 50 percent of the total, for example. And now mortgage bankers and brokers tell us they are being inundated with calls from people who've soured on stocks

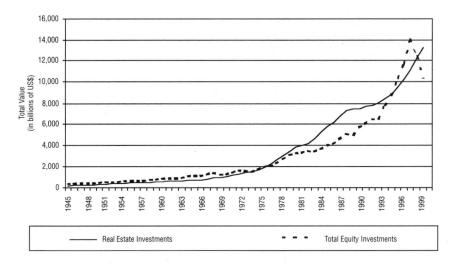

FIGURE I.1   Household Investment in Real Estate and Equities

The investment of households in real estate significantly exceeded that in businesses beginning in 1980. Excluding the five years from 1996 to 2000, real estate has dominated household investment ever since.

Source: Milken Institute. Reprinted with permission.

and are eager to jump into another asset class. We're not here to convince you to dump your stocks. In fact, we still believe that stocks are an excellent vehicle for creating long-term wealth; the present negative sentiment for equities probably signals that the worst may be over. But if you've got cash to invest now and are weary of waiting for the market to solidly rebound, then real estate is an option worth exploring *in addition* to stock investing.

The good news is that real estate makes sense as an investment, regardless of what the stock market is doing. The biggest reason is that when you put money down for commercial or residential property or even a REIT, you diversify the risk of your overall portfolio, reducing the potential that a single investment, bond or stock, can erase all your hard-earned savings. Real estate follows its own cycle, independent of stocks and bonds, and thus serves as a counterweight to your other investments. According to the Chicago-based research firm Ibbotson Associates, properly balanced portfolios not only reduce risk, but enjoy higher returns when a real estate component is added.

That's because real estate investments are three times as likely to maintain their value or even rise when the rest of the market declines. What's more, unlike stock investments, the values of so-called hard assets like real estate actually *improve* with inflation rather than getting nibbled to death by higher prices.

Another persuasive argument for investing in real estate: Returns. Annualized total returns on real estate stand at 9.41 percent since 1977, according to the National Council of Real Estate Investment Fiduciaries. The largest share of that return, income, accounts for 8.05 percent of the gains, while appreciation is 1.2 percent. With long-term forecasts for stock returns now at 9.37 percent, according to Ibbotson, real estate stacks up favorably, and when you add in the tax savings from write-offs, the results are even more encouraging. Of course, results vary by sector, and one of the tricks of investing successfully is finding the right niche to occupy. For example, hotels have been the most lucrative income-producing investments, but also the most volatile, while apartments' steadier results also are less impressive.

Of course, some of the reasons you may decide to invest in real estate may not be strictly quantifiable. Many individuals told me they chose to invest in real estate because they didn't want their hard-earned dollars to become payoff for a greedy CEO who'd decided to use the corporate treasury as a personal piggy bank. To be sure, real estate investing does give the investor ultimate control—and responsibility. It's up to you to pick the right property, estimate cash flows, and pay the right price. You directly manage the investment.

That independence was exactly what appealed to Bill Fletcher when he started investing some 15 years ago in Washington, D.C. At the time, the struggling artist was trying to make ends meet driving a cab. Armed with only a clean credit history, Fletcher started investing in some of the capital city's diciest neighborhoods. He has never owned more than five investment properties, yet he's made a comfortable living all the while because of what he describes as the "ocean of rising prices." These days, his rental units support his art career, allowing him ultimate freedom in what he creates. "I'm still working as an artist," he says. "I've done murals all over the city."

All of those reasons for investing in real estate would exist whether it was 2003 or 2013. But what's compelling about investing in the industry right now is this: While stocks languish under the weight of seemingly dozens of Enron-style embarrassments, the real estate industry went through its own purgatory more than a decade ago. It started back in 1982 when the federal government attempted to stabilize an anemic savings and loan industry by deregulating it. Interest rate ceilings on deposits were removed, lending guidelines were loosened, and thrifts were encouraged to invest liberally in real estate. It worked like a charm—too well, in fact. In the easy credit environment, thrifts lent freely, financing a glut of commercial real estate and creating a raft of bad loans. By the mid-1980s, savings and loans from California to Maryland were failing. (Remember Charles Keating?) It was the era of "see-through" buildings—construction projects that were abandoned midway as the easy money dried up. In 1989, the federal government stepped in with a multibillion-dollar bailout, but the cleanup took years.

The point of bringing up the industry's dirty laundry? Part of the government's solution to the crisis was a tightening of lending regulations. Moreover, bankers became more conservative in their practices. Rafts of scurrilous operators were tossed out. That doesn't mean that there can't be more embarrassing blowups in the future, but for small investors, tired of watching stocks languish as the roundup of rogue CEOs continues, the real estate industry looks like a more even playing field. What's more, the industry's hard-won conservatism meant that instead of feverishly overbuilding during the expansion of the 1990s, the pace of growth was pretty reasonable. The result? Opportunities continue even after the boom years of the 1990s. In our opinion, you can't ask for more than the right opportunity.

In the coming chapters, we'll show you how to take advantage of the options available now, guiding you through the myriad of questions you'll face—from the right way to get financing to how best to renovate your palace. We'll even show you how to sell once you've decided to cash in your investment. These are decisions you really can make on your own—despite what the so-called experts might tell you.

The *SmartMoney* Outlook for Real Estate

Making the most of the advantages that come your way. That's what *SmartMoney* is all about, whether it's stocks, bonds, mutual funds . . . or real estate.

It seems that *everyone* has been making the most of the opportunities in real estate for several years now. They've pushed up the sales volume for single-family homes to record levels, and prices into the stratosphere (see Figure 1.1). Individual investors weren't the Johnny-come-latelies to the real estate boom; they led it. "Real estate is the way to build long-term wealth," says Boston real estate investor Michael Price. In 1985, he and a friend put down $500 to buy a $109,000 apartment house in Brighton, a blue-collar Boston suburb. The two fixed it up and sold it a year later for $245,000.

Those were the days. For while you may be on the lookout for such easy money now, the next decade of real estate investing will likely reward careful, planned investments much more. This chapter will help you get started. We'll begin by demystifying the biggest fear in real estate markets today—the idea that housing prices are a great bubble that is about to burst. We'll share our exclusive guide to the future of home prices, and even open up your horizons with a look at the commercial markets.

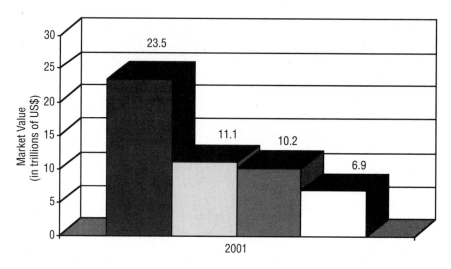

FIGURE 1.1   How Big Is Residential Real Estate?

Valued at over $23 trillion, residential real estate is one of the main asset categories in the United States, easily surpassing the $11 trillion market value of all New York Stock Exchange listed stocks, the $10 trillion value of the country's annual income output, and the $6.9 trillion in assets held by commercial banks.

Source: Milken Institute. Reprinted by permission.

The Great Bubble Debate

Imagine this scenario: Home prices plummet nearly 30 percent over a grisly five-year period. Housing construction grinds to a halt. Foreclosures soar 10 times usual levels. A preview of the nation's housing market? No, it's a description of the worst housing price bust in recent memory: Houston's late 1980s crash, when that energy-dependent Texas city fell into a deep recession after prices for oil plummeted from a high of $40 a barrel to just over $10 in 1986.

The crash hit David Weekley, a homebuilder in Houston at the time, plenty hard. Not only did his business suffer—sales slumped, contracts had to be torn up when buyers lost their jobs, and his business bled red ink of $200,000 a month—but he also ultimately lost his own home, a massive custom house he built himself. So Weekley expanded his business to Dallas, where a more diversified economy stabilized his company and allowed him to survive the recession. Still, it was a close call.

"It was very scary," he says of Houston's debacle. "It was the Depression—and it still affects how I view real estate." Today, Weekley hasn't just survived; he has thrived, moving his business into 14 markets throughout the Southeast. He thinks the possibility of another bust like that of the 1980s is remote at best—at least in Texas. But his experience—and that of Houston itself—is precisely the scenario that so many homeowners and real estate investors across the country fear: a prolonged downturn in home prices that cuts deeply into property values and brings the market to a grinding halt.

Could Houston's experience replay across the country? Not likely. How do we know? First off, with the exception of the Great Depression, housing experts agree that there has never been a nationwide bust of housing prices. The nation's median home values, for example, have risen in each and every year since the National Association of Realtors began keeping records back in 1968. Now, that's not to say that some individual markets, like Houston, haven't experienced periods where prices have declined. But the fact is that if housing prices follow the pattern of previous bubbles, prices would be likely to fall in only a handful of cities—if that. Even at the height of the bubble fear mongering, the nation's most respected home price forecasters, Cambridge, Massachusetts–based Case Shiller Weiss, didn't see any dips at all on the horizon for 52 of the nation's largest metropolitan markets, and that includes places where prices are obviously inflated like San Francisco and Boston. Broadly speaking, the big trend of the past 20 years has been that the only cities vulnerable to a crash are the ones that enjoy the biggest run-ups in the first place; and that largely means coastal cities. They've been cycling about once a decade, so buyer beware. If you're living the heartland, though, you should be able to sleep soundly.

That's not the only reassuring lesson of past bubbles. There's also this: Price bubbles, even monster ones, aren't always followed by price declines. Take California in the early 1980s. The 1981–1982 recession put the brakes on a boom in real estate, but prices never fell despite the fact that interest rates hit 18 percent. The reason was simple:

Homeowners held their houses off the market, waiting for a recovery in prices. "There were very few transactions. Existing home sales and inventories went to record low levels," says Karl Case, Wellesley College economics professor and a research principal and founder of Case Shiller Weiss. Such a scenario, while better than one in which prices plunge, is still no picnic. It means sellers have to stay put, whether or not they lose their jobs or expand their families. Likewise, buyers have few homes from which to choose.

So what does it take for prices to fall? Case is one of the few academics to have written extensively about bubbles and busts, and he believes that the real estate slowdowns don't typically turn into nasty, value-churning busts unless a lot of people lose their jobs, what Case calls "a good economic bang. If the bang is big enough," he says, "prices crack" because incomes can't support new home formation.

Case's research provides two prior examples of big bangs: Los Angeles and Boston on the eve of the 1990–1991 recession. The two cases are different in the way they started—in Boston, the entry-level market caught fire, while in Los Angeles it was the high end that drove the biggest price gains. But in the end, job losses brought both parties to a halt. Before job losses of 5.3 percent (well above the nation's average loss of 2 percent), Los Angelinos had enjoyed home price appreciation of 102.4 percent in just five years. The losses? When the firecracker fizzled, prices fell 21.9 percent. Likewise, Boston, after enjoying appreciation of 158.9 percent in the late 1980s, experienced dramatic job cuts of 11.6 percent during the recession as prices tumbled nearly 16 percent (see Figure 1.2). Notice something else about both of these examples? Neither of the busts comes anywhere close to erasing all the gains of the boom.

In the current cycle, few of the nation's metropolitan areas have witnessed price appreciation anything close to that of Boston or Los Angeles in the late 1980s, according to figures from the Office of Federal Housing Enterprise. The closest are a handful of coastal cities in California and in the Northeast. The biggest gainer from the past five years is Santa Cruz, California, where prices are up 89.3 percent over the past five years. Other California cities with eye-popping gains: Oakland, up 82.6 percent; Salinas, up 81.3 percent; Santa

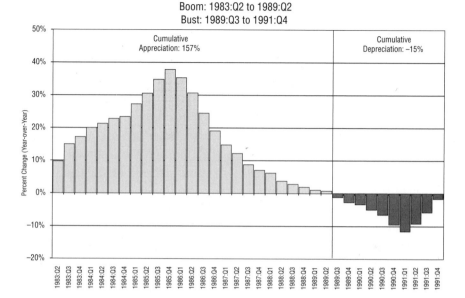

FIGURE 1.2   Boston Home Prices—Boom and Bust
Source: Fiserv CSW, Inc., Cambridge, Massachusetts, www.cswcasa.com.

Rosa, 81.3 percent; and Santa Barbara, 81.2 percent. On the East Coast, Boston's five-year prices rose 73 percent, and suburban feeder cities such as Lowell and Lawrence were up 74.3 percent and 72.7 percent respectively. New York's price appreciation pales by comparison, up just 60 percent.

But combine the price appreciation data with job losses and the outlook becomes darker for a handful of cities. In San Francisco and San Jose in particular, employment over the two years ending in July 2002 is down 4.9 percent and 6.1 percent respectively. New York suburbs like Stamford, Connecticut, are off 3.5 percent during the same period, and Boston is off 1.4 percent. In traditional manufacturing cities like Detroit, where employment is off 4.4 percent, the recession's pain is evident as well.

You'd think that would allow you to forecast with confidence that prices would decline in those areas. But the one commonality that ties each of the previous boom/busts together is that prices, when they're on a roll moving higher, eventually stop selling on the fundamentals—the location, size, and condition of the home—and instead sell on buyers' irrational belief that no matter what they pay, prices will continue to go higher. (Does this sound like a familiar scenario to you stock investors out there?)

Case is one prognosticator who's been forced to restate his expectations higher as home prices have defied expectations. "We've been forecasting a slowdown for a year and a half and it hasn't materialized," he says. "You can safely say prices are high and there have to be adjustments over time—but you don't know how long it takes," he says. What's more, as the game of musical chairs comes to an end, most potential sellers will opt, if they can, to wait out the market rather than sell and risk a lower price. And that's exactly what Case has come to decide will happen this time around. Like California in the 1980s, prices are most likely to flatten out for a while, before resuming their inevitable march higher.

The Long-Term Outlook

Short-term moves in real estate prices can have big consequences for investors, but the real question is: What's going to happen over the long haul? After all, that's generally what most investors (the smart ones, anyway) are signing up for when they invest in real estate in the first place. To get a handle on the future direction of the market, we started by compiling a load of data, including regional economic information from Economy.com, the Meyers Group, and Woods & Poole. We gave each market zero to 10 points in each of the following categories: housing affordability trends; future building permits; predicted job growth; and recession resistance (in other words, how many quarters out of the next 10 are expected to bring good employment news). A city's vacancy rate and income level were each worth zero to five points, as were demographic changes in each market: Are typical 35- to 49-year-old homebuyers coming or going? Check out the results in Table 1.1. As you'll see, the ideal city—meaning all factors are as favorable as possible—gets a score of 100. Markets with a score of 60 and above are primed for price appreciation; those below

TABLE 1.1 SMARTMONEY HOME PRICE OUTLOOK

Score	Metropolitan Area	Affordability	Building Permits	Employment	Recession Resistance	Vacancy Rate	Income Level	Population
73.4	Greensboro–Winston-Salem–High Point, NC	9	9	10	8	3	2	3
72.5	Nashville, TN	9	10	6	10	3	2	4
70.1	Greenville-Spartanburg-Anderson, SC	8	8	8	10	4	2	3
67.0	Norfolk–Virginia Beach–Newport News, VA–NC	10	9	6	8	3	1	3
66.8	Birmingham, AL	9	9	5	10	3	1	3
66.3	Fort Worth–Arlington, TX	8	9	6	8	4	2	3
65.7	Las Vegas, NV–AZ	8	6	7	10	3	1	5
65.4	Tucson, AZ	7	6	9	8	4	2	3
65.1	Richmond-Petersburg, VA	7	10	6	8	4	1	3
64.9	San Antonio, TX	7	8	5	10	4	2	2
64.7	Atlanta, GA	6	8	10	6	3	1	4
64.5	Grand Rapids-Muskegon-Holland, MI	7	8	7	8	4	1	3
64.5	Salt Lake City-Ogden, UT	9	9	8	6	3	1	2
64.2	Phoenix-Mesa, AZ	6	7	10	8	3	1	4
62.8	Cleveland-Lorain-Elyria, OH	8	9	8	6	4	2	1
61.3	Houston, TX	5	8	5	10	4	2	2
60.2	Louisville, KY–IN	8	9	6	6	4	1	2
60.2	Dallas, TX	8	7	6	8	3	2	2
60.1	Jacksonville, FL	7	10	2	10	4	0	3
60.0	Pittsburgh, PA	8	8	4	8	4	2	1

(Continued)

TABLE 1.1 (Continued)

Score	Metropolitan Area	Affordability	Building Permits	Employment	Recession Resistance	Vacancy Rate	Income Level	Population
59.8	Charlotte-Gastonia-Rock Hill, NC–SC	8	8	6	6	3	1	4
59.7	Raleigh-Durham-Chapel Hill, NC	9	8	6	6	0	2	5
59.5	Portland–Vancouver, OR–WA	9	7	8	8	2	0	2
59.2	Providence-Warwick-Pawtucket, RI	6	8	3	10	4	1	3
59.2	Columbus, OH	7	8	6	8	3	1	3
59.0	Washington, DC–MD–VA	7	7	3	10	4	1	3
58.9	Orlando, FL	5	8	6	8	4	1	4
58.5	Austin–San Marcos, TX	6	1	9	10	3	1	4
58.4	Indianapolis, IN	8	10	6	4	3	1	3
58.3	Oklahoma City, OK	7	10	4	10	3	1	0
57.6	Cincinnati, OH–KY–IN	7	9	6	6	3	1	2
57.4	West Palm Beach–Boca Raton, FL	9	8	0	8	3	1	5
57.3	Milwaukee-Waukesha, WI	7	9	6	6	4	1	1
57.2	Chicago, IL	8	9	6	6	4	1	2
56.7	Tulsa, OK	7	9	3	10	4	1	1
56.6	Minneapolis–St. Paul, MN	5	8	5	8	5	1	2
56.6	Los Angeles–Long Beach, CA	5	8	5	8	4	1	2
56.3	Detroit, MI	6	7	10	4	4	2	2
55.8	Miami, FL	4	10	2	10	4	1	3
55.5	Dayton-Springfield, OH	8	10	6	4	4	1	1

55.3	Nassau-Suffolk, NY	5	10	2	8	5	2	2
55.2	Memphis, TN–AR–MS	7	8	6	4	3	2	3
55.0	Riverside–San Bernardino, CA	3	8	1	10	4	2	5
54.4	Middlesex-Somerset-Hunterdon, NJ	6	7	4	8	4	1	3
53.9	Philadelphia, PA–NJ	9	8	5	8	4	1	2
53.6	Hartford, CT	7	8	6	4	4	1	2
53.4	Bergen-Passaic, NJ	6	9	6	4	4	1	2
53.3	Sacramento, CA	3	8	1	10	4	3	4
52.7	Saint Louis, MO–IL	7	9	6	4	4	1	1
52.4	Kansas City, MO–KS	6	9	3	8	3	1	2
51.3	New York, NY	5	9	4	6	4	1	2
51.2	Omaha, NE–IA	7	9	5	4	4	1	1
50.6	New Orleans, LA	7	9	5	4	3	2	0
50.0	Honolulu, HI	7	8	3	8	4	0	0
49.7	Seattle-Bellevue-Everett, WA	5	7	8	2	4	2	2
49.2	San Diego, CA	1	7	2	10	4	1	4
48.2	Orange County, CA	1	6	2	10	4	2	3
48.0	Tampa–St. Petersburg–Clearwater, FL	5	10	0	8	3	1	2
46.9	Denver, CO	4	7	7	6	3	1	0
46.3	Baltimore, MD	5	8	3	4	3	2	3
44.7	Boston, MA–NH	0	7	5	6	4	2	3
43.6	Fort Lauderdale, FL	4	6	1	8	3	1	3
43.2	Oakland, CA	3	5	2	8	4	2	3
39.8	San Jose, CA	3	0	8	6	4	1	3
37.2	San Francisco, CA	3	2	6	4	5	1	1

Source: Woods & Poule Economics, Inc., Washington, D.C.; Economy.com, Inc.; and the Meyers Group.

13

50 may see values erode. Between 50 and 60, stability reigns. Keep in mind that the life of this particular chart is just three years.

Now, you're no doubt wondering how it is that a bunch of mid-size Southern cities came out on top. Credit our strong belief that the recession will ultimately melt away and be replaced by recovery. Since manufacturing was the sector hardest hit in the downturn, it's likely to be the first to recover. "The most significant rebound will come in manufacturing centers, including areas like the Carolinas and parts of the industrial Midwest," says Mark Zandi, chief economist at Economy.com. "Areas that are more dependent on technology and financial services will take longer to recover more fully, such as California, Denver, New York, and Boston." Other areas to do well early on include Washington, D.C., the only entity with an open pocketbook, and parts of Florida, which is benefiting from investment inflows from Latin America.

In the longer run, home prices will be driven higher in markets where companies and workforces are located that contribute to health care of the aging boomers and the education of their children and grandchildren. Watch for continued strength in the corridor between central New Jersey and Washington, D.C., where many important pharmaceutical, biotech, and medical instrumentation companies and health care institutions make their homes, from Merck in central New Jersey to the National Institutes of Health in Bethesda, Maryland.

California will continue to post strong growth in the long run due to its status as an immigration state, rather than because of its leadership in technology. Watch for other western states to enjoy home price gains too, as retirees flood states like Nevada and Arizona, and businesses migrate east to escape California's high prices.

Cycles within Cycles

Have you missed it? That's what a lot of people mulling an investment in real estate are thinking. They see the appreciation in home values of the past decade and figure that the big money has already been made. Buying now, they reason, would be like buying Internet stocks in the spring of 2000. While it's true that the price you pay for your real estate investment may be the single biggest determinant of your success (in that way it's not so different from stock investing), you need to think a little more broadly. That's because there is more than just the single-family home sector in the real estate investing sea. Each property segment from office to retail to apartments has its own boom-and-bust cycle that often does not coincide with what's going on in single-family homes. What's more, contrary to the ebb and flow of the residential housing market, commercial cycles can be far more abrupt, marching in lockstep with the economy's ups and downs while the trajectory of home prices is gentler. And it's those downturns or pauses in commercial real estate that serve as openings for newcomers eager to invest.

Granted, you're not likely to buy an entire office building à la Donald Trump and the other moguls. Still, you might consider other types of commercial property that fit your pocketbook and your management capabilities. Here are the major ones.

Office

This sector feels the impact from the economy's moves most keenly since the health of businesses that lease space is tied directly to the pace of economic growth. For that reason, the 2001 recession hit office markets hard. The tech boom fueled office development through the late 1990s, especially along the coasts, in the San Francisco Bay area, Boston, and Washington, D.C. Denver, home to several telecom companies, including Qwest Communications, also expanded. When technology companies hit a wall in 2000, some of the office space was subleased to other tenants, and vacancy rates, one measure of the real estate industry's health, held pretty solid—for a while. But the recession of 2001 drove even the sublets out, pushing vacancies higher—to 16 percent nationwide, according to Torto Wheaton Research.

The Boston area is a good example of the pain felt by these onetime market leaders. As companies like EMC Corporation, the data storage maker, laid off thousands of people, the suburban office market along the Route 128 corridor sank. Vacancies spiked to 30 and 35 percent.

But that wasn't the only problem for the region. In the downtown where investment banks and mutual fund families make their homes, vacancies soared to 12 percent in 2002—the highest in seven years—as the bear market for stocks took its toll. "The office market is very soft," says Ed Riekstins, president of New England Realty Resources and a commercial mortgage broker. "The tenants are in command."

It's not just the financial and tech capitals that have suffered in this downturn. In Indiana, where manufacturing and steel industries have slumped, the market is anemic. "We're not worried about the real estate market popping like a bubble," says Mike Petrie, president of P/R Mortgage & Investment Corp. "We're just trying to get a little air in the bag."

To be sure, though, the real estate market, even the office segment, is driven by the local economy. And that means there are pockets of strength that some investors are taking advantage of. "Right now is one of the best cycles I've ever seen," says Michael Rauckman, who gave up work as an accountant several years ago to invest in real estate full-time. Rauckman, who lives in Belleville, Illinois, a suburb of Saint Louis, owns 32 properties, including individual homes he rents out, retail stores, and office space. One of his best-performing properties recently has been an office condominium that he bought and finished himself. Because he did the work on his own, his costs are lower than those of others in the same complex, which allows him to pocket a nice profit each month. His costs are just $7 a square foot, and neighbors are charging $12 a square foot. "The condo office is great," he says. "I'm coming out ahead."

So how do you find such pockets? If your region's market is plagued by high vacancies and sluggish rent growth, you'll want to bide your time until the pressure on owners becomes so severe that they have to think about selling. In other words, you'll bottom fish for good deals just like value investors in the stock market look for bargains. That's what Michael Price's company, Eastport Real Estate Services in Waltham, Massachusetts, was doing back in mid-2002. "We want to swoop in and pick up stuff," he says. The key to success? Not overpaying. Even by mid-2002, according to Price, office building owners in the Boston area were clinging to higher valuations that made sense at the top of the market. Remember, office building prices are a direct reflection of lease values. To keep from overpaying you'll need to make sure you know the value of those leases. (Read Chapter 4 for a more detailed methodology.)

Price and others believe that this particular downturn is likely to be less severe than others because there's been less overbuilding than in previous cycles. Barring a double-dip recession, recovery to more normal levels is expected by mid-2003, with complete recovery for the sector by 2004. That's bad news if you have to sell a big office building in the heart of the downturn—but good news if you're shopping for one. The best options for small investors are office condos such as Rauckman bought and small suburban buildings, perhaps the one that houses your own business.

Retail

The strength of consumer spending kept shopping malls and strip centers from going the way of the office market in the 2001 recession. But there's been a big change in the way the retail market works. The big malls have become pretty much the exclusive domain of large REITs dedicated to regional and superregional mall development, like Simon Property Group. Smaller investors have found solid profits, however, in neighborhood centers, particularly those that are anchored by a grocery store. "The food and beverage sectors are the mainstay of the neighborhood centers, and margins in that business have been increasing steadily throughout the 1990s as food prices have declined," says Jim Costello, a senior economist at Torto Wheaton Research, a Boston-based provider of commercial real estate data.

What's more, these retail outlets should continue to perform well even if consumer spending were to weaken, since their wares are essentials. Even the tenants that typically surround the big grocers and drugstores, such as pizza parlors, postal service chain stores, and others, are more recession resistant than their more upscale cousins. Whatever you do, though, you'll want to make sure your tenants have the wherewithal to withstand any short-lived spending slowdown.

Jane Garvey, a Chicago real estate investor, got started investing in single-family homes with her husband, and made it a full-time job back in 1983. In all that time, she's bought just one commercial building, a storefront whose longtime tenant ran a pet treat business. Eager to expand, but short on cash, she convinced Garvey to buy the building and lease it back to her. "The plan worked great—for her," Garvey recalls. Quickly outgrowing the space, the tenant sold a portion of her business—dog grooming—to another business operator, and moved the successful outfit to another location. The second tenant failed miserably, filing for bankruptcy and leaving behind a $2,200 water bill and an infestation of cockroaches. "It was a nightmare," remembers Garvey, who to this day continues to stick to apartments and homes.

Apartments

No doubt rental properties, apartments, and even single-family homes are the preferred starting point for most investors eager to get into real estate investing. And it's no surprise why. First off, individual investors feel most comfortable investing in properties that are similar to what they already own—homes. What's more, bankers are likely to be freer with capital in this category since multifamily apartment owners are seldom delinquent on loans and rent trends are steady, says Gail Davis Cardwell, senior vice president at Mortgage Bankers Association.

That's where Michael Price, now a real estate professional, started his career in the early 1980s. After graduating from college, he worked in the city's Back Bay neighborhood scraping wallpaper and painting multifamily homes. He quickly was hooked, and started buying condos to make some extra money after he got his first job. In 2002, he sold the last of those properties, a Brighton condo he bought in 1983 for $35,000. The price he got? $210,000. "I never thought when I bought it that 19 years later we'd be cashing out, resulting in such a huge gain," he says. "It goes to show you if you hold real estate long-term, you're going to build wealth."

What's more, now is an unusually good time to think about investing in the rental market. To understand why, you need to know how the apartment industry has been changing. Basically, the market for apartments has broken into three different segments: There are the people who make about half the median income and receive federal assistance in paying their rents. At the high end, there is a market of people who want luxury accommodations. And then there is the broad middle, people whose incomes are 60 to 90 percent of the median and who can't afford the rents in brand-new buildings.

"The overall rental production during the 1990s dropped off substantially from the 1970 and 1980s. If you look at what was produced, it looks like a barbell," says John McIlwain, a senior resident fellow at the Urban Land Institute. "At one end there is a lot of production of low-income housing properties. At the other end there is an increasing number of luxury properties for people who would prefer to rent even though they can afford to buy. What is going on today is . . . [that] the middle group—the bread and butter of the industry . . . teachers, office assistants, paralegals, tech workers—can't afford to pay the rent and the housing isn't getting built. There is a huge market for rental housing that the rental housing industry can't serve."

And that means opportunity for small investors who are uniquely suited to manage homes or small multifamily properties that can sop up demand among middle-tier renters. "The big boys aren't interested in this area," says Dorcas Cecil, founder of a management firm that bears her name. "I have some clients who are builders and developers, and trying to get the numbers to work with what you can get for rent is difficult. It's an opportunity for the little guy."

Another reason that rental units makes sense? Population growth. According to McIlwain, the next two decades will bring population growth that will mimic the baby boom of the 1950s, a 28-million-person population bulge. In this decade, the United States will add an additional 25 to 30 million people through immigration and internal growth. "Where are these people going to live?" he asks. "We're in an incredible population boom. The industry can't build fast enough. We don't have an overhang of built but unsold homes on the market. The existing home market is tight. You'll find the housing industry won't provide the housing it used to in the late 1960s, early 1970s, and 1980s."

Industrial

Warehouse space is another segment, like office, that is faced with excess capacity. "Lots of new space is coming on line," says Torto Wheaton's Costello. This space is the quick-change artist of the real estate industry. Elements of the building are constructed away from the site, shipped there, and slapped together quickly. That flexibility takes some of the speculative nature out of the sector. "A number of our clients were thinking it's the safe sector," he says. "Instead, performance has gotten out of whack with high availability." One potential saving grace? Tenants are opting for newer buildings that are more efficient to operate.

Industrial is a specialized market, though. Only experienced investors ought to apply, because its speculative nature makes it dangerous for investing newcomers.

2

WHAT EVERY INVESTOR SHOULD KNOW ABOUT REAL ESTATE AGENTS

For most of us, buying a home is our single biggest purchase—ever. Unless you're lucky enough to inherit a home or buy one directly from an owner, chances are you'll work with a real estate agent. That's because real estate agents are the industry's gatekeepers. Every year, agents assist in more than five million transactions, showing properties to potential buyers, marketing new listings with open houses, and placing ads online and in newspapers. Many recommend mortgage brokers and lawyers to assist in the closings.

They're especially helpful to first-time buyers and sellers, who may be nervous about what to expect from this big transaction they're about to pull off and need a bit of hand-holding. But even many seasoned homeowners swear by their agents, happily delegating to someone else all those annoying little details you have to worry about when buying or selling a home.

Still, there's a huge difference between good agents and bad ones. Hire the wrong one and you will seriously regret it. Some, for instance, are the type who insist on making you trudge through all the neighborhood white elephants—the homes that can't be sold because they have 1970s-style kitchens or unusual layouts that require you to walk through the bathroom to get to the master bedroom. They're hoping that maybe, just maybe, you'll be desperate enough to buy one of these lemons.

Some agents are obsessed with getting you to snap up a house as quickly as you might pick out a sack of groceries, so they can get paid faster. Like the real estate agent in Independence, Missouri, who convinced a couple of first-time buyers not to have the roof of the home they were intent on buying inspected. Her reasoning? A disclosure form from the owners stated that the roof was less than two years old. So the couple bought the home—without inspection—only to find that the rafters were sagging and the whole roof was in danger of collapsing. As it turned out, the only thing new about the roof was the shingles, says Max Gordon, an Overland Park, Kansas, real estate agent and attorney who testified in the case when it ended up in court.

When Jason Robbins and his wife were looking for a home in Austin, Texas, several years ago, the two intended to buy an older home with character and charm. But their agent, a motherly type who was full of advice for the young couple, steered them toward a house in a spanking new development. "She wanted to put us in a new cracker box house—a tract house," he remembers. Eventually, the two novices relented and decided to buy one. Robbins was surprised, though, when they went to negotiate for the house, that the agent, who'd been full of suggestions, was nowhere to be found. The couple undertook the most intimidating part of the process of buying a new home—negotiating the sale price—on their own. It wasn't until later that Robbins learned that the agent got an extra bonus—a 4 percent commission rather than 3—by selling them the suburban tract house, incentive enough to make her ignore the couple's wishes. "She wasn't looking out for our best interests," says Robbins.

The next time the couple hit the housing market they spent as much time picking an agent as they did a house. The strategy paid off—big time. They quickly located the house of their dreams, a three-bedroom, two-and-a-half-bath house on a corner half-acre lot dotted with trees, says Robbins. The pair—and their children—were charmed by the older home's little idiosyncrasies like the closet under the stairs. Says Robbins, "There's something intangible to a twenty-year-old house—it has soul."

Having found a house her clients liked, the agent went to work checking out how long the house had been on the market (six months) and how many offers were outstanding (none). Her close review of the property revealed that the house needed some upgrading, such as replacement of the kitchen floor and other superficial work. But all were changes the Robbinses felt comfortable with. Sensing that the buyers might be anxious to sell, the agent recommended bidding well below the asking price. The couple ended up getting the house $20,000 below asking. "It worked out the way she predicted—she was very experienced," says Robbins.

That's the kind of agent that knowledgeable real estate investors count on. Before you can pick the right agent for your needs, though, you've got to understand the basics of how brokers work and the many conflicts inherent in any real estate deal. Without that understanding, you'll risk sabotaging your own house search or sale—for it's often to the real estate agent's advantage for these details to be left unexplained. Following are 10 things you absolutely need to know about real estate agents before hiring one.

NO. 1: YOUR AGENT DOESN'T REALLY WORK FOR YOU.

The first and most important question to ask any agent—Who are you working for?—is deceptively simple and rarely asked by most buyers. Let's face it; if you're like most people the way you'll pick your agent is by calling the phone number at the top of a For Sale sign of that dream home you've seen as you whizzed by at 40 miles an hour. Pretty soon you find yourself being ferried around by the agent, who asks about your needs, laughs at your jokes, and sympathizes with your shock at home prices. It's no surprise, then, that you end up forgetting whom you're dealing with. The fact is, most agents and brokers are not really working for the homebuyers—they're working for the *sellers*. And any info you pass on to the agent goes right into the ear of the buyer.

"Legally brokers are required to provide their sellers with any information that can help them get the best possible prices for their homes," says Stephen Israel, president of Buyer's Edge, a Bethesda, Maryland–based company that represents homebuyers rather than sellers. So, if you share the strategy of your offer with the agent— let's say you want to make an initial offer of $450,000 but you're willing to pay $500,000—count on that information being passed right on to the seller. Even the details of your bank loan preap- proval—the fact that the bank will lend you far more than you want to pay—become part of the data that's shared with the seller.

NO. 2: YOUR AGENT MAY HAVE HIDDEN INCENTIVES FOR SELLING YOU CERTAIN PROPERTIES.

When Mark Bradshaw was looking for a place to live in Boston after being hired by Harvard Business School as an associate professor, he had a funny feeling about the agent who was showing him properties. "I couldn't help but think she was only showing me houses that her company had on the market," he recalls. When he pointedly asked her if that were true, she sheepishly admitted it was. "We exchanged that look of two people who are never going to see each other again," says Bradshaw, who dropped her in favor of an agent who would show him homes put on the market by rivals as well as her own brokerage's listings. The whole business, though, left a bad taste in his mouth.

No issue is more confusing for buyers than what most states call "dual agency." That means that one real estate agency, sometimes one agent, is representing both the buyer and the seller in a transaction. The problem is particularly commonplace in small markets where it's not unusual to find just one or two brokerages selling properties. Agents love this kind of deal because it increases the amount of com- mission they can earn—instead of having to split the usual 6 percent commission with an outsider, the entire commission remains inside the agency. In addition, for the agent representing the buyer there's of- ten an additional bonus paid for keeping the whole deal in-house. "Dual agency is a huge problem," says Israel. He maintains that the practice introduces a host of conflicts of interest. "Let's assume we're three weeks out from settlement and a tree hits the house," he says. "The seller says, 'I'll fix it.' The buyer says, 'I don't want it fixed—because I don't want to buy the house.' The contract says the property will be conveyed in substantially the same condition. But who determines that? Who's the broker going to side with? If you want out of the deal, your agent can't advocate against the person sitting next to them in the office."

NO. 3: EVEN A BUYER'S AGENT HAS AN INCENTIVE TO MAKE SURE YOU PAY THE MOST FOR YOUR NEW HOME.

Okay, so let's assume you've opted to use a buyer's agent, rather than a conventional agent or dual agent. Are your problems with conflicts solved? Unfortunately, no. Unless you've agreed to pay the broker a flat fee for helping you find a home, even buyer's brokers are working on commission—and therefore have a financial interest to make sure the buyer pays the highest price possible.

Worse, some brokers who represent themselves as buyer's advocates are working for companies that represent sellers and pay the buyer's brokers big bonuses. If you want to make sure your buyer's agent is working solely on your behalf, check out www.naeba.com, the web site of the National Association of Exclusive Buyer Agents (NAEBA). Members pledge to help their clients get the lowest price possible, and some even work on a flat fee structure rather than a commission.

NO. 4: AGENTS' PAY IS NEGOTIABLE.

Real estate agents act as if the 6 percent commission—usually split 50–50 between the buyer's agent and the seller's agent—is carved in stone. Far from it. "Price fixing is illegal," says Bradley Inman, founder of HomeGain.com, which matches buyers and sellers. "You can't fix commission prices." Even in red-hot markets, brokers may be convinced to discount their commissions when demand is high for good properties.

Another way to get a bargain on commissions is to interview

several agents and get them to bid against each other. Commission size was just one issue Tami Dean had when she and her husband wanted to sell their Lawrenceville, Georgia, home in just 30 days so the two could take new jobs in a Houston suburb. Trying to short-cut the usual months-long process, Dean signed up with Home-Gain.com. She received proposals from a dozen agents—one offering to charge a commission of just 3.5 percent. She interviewed by telephone a handful of the salespeople, selecting one who charged a slightly higher commission, 5 percent, but who also would promote her property in local magazines and newspapers. Within eight days Dean had two solid offers, and two weeks later the house was sold.

"I've moved several times, and it was the best move I've ever had," she says.

NO. 5: AN OPEN HOUSE MAY NOT BE
THE BEST WAY TO MARKET YOUR HOME.

Hire a real estate broker to sell your home, and one of the first things he'll likely suggest is hosting an open house so potential buyers and brokers can casually check out your property on some weekend afternoon. While it's promoted as a great way of finding a buyer, a National Association of Realtors study found that the success rate for open houses is a mere 2 percent.

No matter. The open house serves another important purpose—for the broker, according to Sean McNeill, an independent real estate broker based in New York City who spoke with *SmartMoney* magazine about the topic. "It gives him a database of clients. When you have an open house, you get all kinds of people walking in. Some are looking at homes for sale to see how much they should sell their places for; others are actually looking for much smaller or larger homes but want to get a look at what's out there." Both of these kinds of people are perfect pickings for a broker looking to increase his roster of buyers and sellers. "Think about it: The broker is devoting a couple of hours to this on a weekend. He won't do that unless it helps him in a big way."

NO. 6: YOUR AGENT MAY FAIL TO SHOW YOU ALL THE OFFERS FOR YOUR HOME.

Legally, the broker you hire to sell your home is obligated to tell you about all the offers that come in. In reality, some brokers don't. Perhaps he thinks the offer is insultingly low for you, but more likely "the broker thinks it's too low for his own purposes. He wants to hold out for a bigger commission," says Sean McNeill. Or else there's an outside broker (or "cobroker") circling your house, and the primary broker is waiting for another of his own clients to make an offer, so he can keep the 6 percent commission for himself.

"You must be clear with your broker that you want to be informed of all offers," McNeill says. "Otherwise you may be leaving him to make the kinds of decisions that you should be making." To protect yourself: Check the listing agreement drawn up when you hire the broker; if the promise to disclose all offers isn't listed explicitly, insist that it be added.

NO. 7: YOU SHOULDN'T RELY ON YOUR AGENT FOR ADVICE THAT'S OUTSIDE HIS OR HER RANGE OF EXPERTISE.

Real estate agents love to suggest big ideas to prospective buyers, like moving the driveway or combining the dining and living rooms into one great room. But one buyer who took such advice lived to regret it. Manhattan-based architect Mary Langan told *SmartMoney* that one of her clients who had bought a dilapidated house with a beautiful piece of property on a marshland was told by his broker that the sleepy little town wouldn't care what he did with the property. So he sank thousands into a backyard shed, pulled down trees, and filled in some of the marshland. Now the town is making him comply with environmental regulations and put most of it back the way it was.

Likewise, Max Gordon, an Overland Park, Kansas, real estate broker and attorney, says he often sees brokers penning in clauses to real estate transactions. "I see [brokers] pushing the envelope all the time with amendments and addenda," he says. "They draft language that can have consequences without really understanding it—but they want to keep the sale going."

For example, Gordon says, it's fairly common for a "transaction to close on one day but possession doesn't happen until a later date, in which case the buyer rents the house back to the seller for those days." Gordon warns that a couple of lines penned by your broker in a contract isn't enough to clear up who's responsible for any damage in the interim. If a clause is worded improperly, you as the buyer could end up liable for damage done by your "rental tenant." The same goes for the purchases of non–real estate items (such as patio furniture) and owner carryback (in which the seller provides some of the financing). "In both cases payment terms might not get spelled out clearly," Gordon says, "and can result in one party taking advantage of the other." Whether you're the buyer or the seller, get the offer contract reviewed by your lawyer before you sign. "You have to be prepared for the worst-case scenario," says Gordon.

NO. 8: YOUR AGENT'S WEB SITE MAY BE A TOTAL TIME WASTER.

The Web would seem like the perfect shortcut when shopping for a house. The Internet can deliver a good deal of information on homes in real time, even short movies of new listings, making it a perfect search tool. In fact, over half of the homebuyers looking for a new dream house go to the Internet to conduct their search, according to the National Association of Realtors. But some brokers' sites are better than others, and you need to look beyond a well-designed home page to figure that out.

One common flaw: posting houses that sold long ago. While the mistake can be simple negligence, others think that it's a bait-and-switch type ploy. "It brings people in, but it gets them upset when they find out that the property's [gone]," says Frank D'Ostilio Jr., president of William Orange Realty in the New Haven, Connecticut, area.

In addition to checking up on a web site's prominent listings, sellers should make sure the site is kept current. Active sites will change their photographs weekly. "If you look one week and next week and there are not changes, it's a good sign the web site isn't being updated," says Roger Lautt, a Chicago-based broker with RE/MAX Exclusive Properties, who has had a web site for the past five years.

Check, too, to make sure that the site is easy to navigate. "You want a broker who keeps himself relatively high on search engines," adds Lautt, whose own webmaster makes sure his site is hooked in with Realtor.com, Yahoo!, and the RE/MAX site. The site also should have plenty of links to school boards of education, commuter transportation schedules, and park departments, among others. "One of the big things a broker should have is community information," he says.

NO. 9: YOU MAY NOT NEED A REAL ESTATE AGENT AT ALL.

Brokers want you to think you can't buy a house without them, but in fact it's not that hard to do. Almost every community has some sort of "for sale by owner" publication or web site dedicated to matching buyers and sellers directly. And, if your area doesn't have such references, there's always the classified ads and For Sale by Owner yard signs. Finding the homes usually isn't a problem, but culling the ones that are really appealing is a more difficult task. Remember: The old adage that owners only sell properties that the pros can't is sometimes true. So, to save time be sure to check out the locations of these homes before you set up an appointment. (Does the property overlook the commuter rail station? Is it located on a busy highway?)

Once you get started looking at some of these properties, you may find the process more appealing than working with an agent. In fact, you'll find some real advantages to buying directly from the seller—the biggest being the potential for a lower price. "You stand to save money because the seller didn't have to inflate their price to cover the commission," says Antoinette Supple, co-owner of *Picket Fence Preview*, a monthly magazine that publishes ads for homes for sale by their owners.

Another advantage, says Supple, is that buyers don't find themselves the victim of a listing agent who is holding out for a sale to a buyer who is a client of the agency. "The listing agency always wants the entire 6 percent commission," says Supple. "You shouldn't have to go to every listing agency to beat the system."

Finally, buyers may well get more detailed information about the property directly from sellers. "The owner can tell you where the school bus stops, and where the hiking trails in the neighborhood are," she says. "It's the little things people really care about when they move into a house."

Intimidated by the prospect of buying without an agent? After all, who's going to take care of all that paperwork associated with a purchase? The fact of the matter is that even without a real estate agent there will be plenty of professionals involved who will be pushing to get the deal closed—like the mortgage broker, your bank's lawyer, and your attorney.

NO. 10: THE REAL ESTATE INDUSTRY IS LIGHTLY REGULATED.

You'd think that the real estate industry would have loads of regulators circling its practitioners. After all, hundreds of thousands of dollars are at stake in nearly every transaction. Wish it were so. The main watchdogs, the Association of Real Estate License Law Officials (ARELLO), a group of state regulators, focuses on setting educational standards for and licensing agents, not necessarily holding their feet to the fire. What's more, their offices are often short staffed and underfunded. Of the 2.3 million licensed agents in the country, only 426 had their licenses revoked by regulators in 2000, or just a fraction of 1 percent. "When you buy a stock, the people handling your investment are highly regulated," says HomeGain's Bradley Inman. "But when you're selling a house you're literally handing over your biggest asset to someone who has no local or federal regulations. The bar is set very low."

What's more, required education may be pretty minimal. Most states require 30 to 90 hours of classroom time and passage of a test, which mostly covers the language of real estate, before awarding a real estate license, says ARELLO executive vice president Craig Cheatham. Agents learn the subtleties of sales and marketing on the job—a fact that makes picking an experienced agent all the more important.

You can check to see whether your agent is licensed by accessing a site maintained by the National Association of Realtors at www.arello.com. Contact your state board to make sure the agent has not been censured or reprimanded by regulators. You can find contact numbers for regulatory agencies at both www.arello.com and www.arello.org.

3

RESEARCHING THE MARKET

uying a new home can be one of the most exhilarating—and
frustrating—things you'll ever do. You search the ads, tour a
handful of new homes, and before you know it you're bidding
for what you hope will become your family's refuge for years to
come. In the momentum that develops around almost any real estate
search, it's all too easy to forget what's at risk. Sure, there's the consid-
erable nest egg you've scraped together as a down payment hanging in
the balance. But your decision will also likely determine the quality of
your children's education, your future wealth—in short, nothing less
than your family's happiness. Even if you're buying a home as an investment, not a residence, the property you choose will be critical to
your financial future.

Ever wonder why buyers suffer from post-purchase trauma, fret-
ting over every detail? It's because the average homebuyer looks at just
10 properties before putting down his or her hard-earned cash, according to a poll conducted by the National Association of Realtors.
Moving at warp speed nearly ensures that you'll wake up nights worrying whether you could've done better, wondering whether you've
paid too much or if you snapped up a real lemon.

People looking for investment property aren't necessarily any more deliberate. When Stephen Craffen, a Fair Lawn, New Jersey, financial adviser, made his first real estate investment back in 1981—an eight-family apartment building in Union City—he moved way too fast. "I was 23 and eager to buy a property," he recalls. "The money I had was burning a hole in my pocket." Craffen put down nearly every penny of his savings—$15,000—as a down payment on the $75,000 building, deciding to skip a property inspection in his rush to close the deal. Three months later, the boiler blew and Craffen faced an $8,000 bill to fix it, forcing the young real estate investor to borrow money from his father and take out a second mortgage on the property. "I wasn't knowledgeable, and I didn't realize that something like that can break," he says. "I was naive." Adding insult to injury, he found the heating cost estimates given him by the owner were 30 percent lower than they should have been. Craffen managed to recover from the mess financially, mainly because of tax breaks that no longer exist, but it changed forever the way he does business. These days, Craffen moves more deliberately, hiring a mechanical engineer to inspect properties he's thinking of buying and requiring sellers to provide copies of fuel bills so he can check out their claims.

But it's not just the speed with which buyers move that's a problem. Plenty of folks take their time searching for properties, asking questions along the way. The trouble is they rely on a single source—a real estate agent or a best friend—for information that person may be ill prepared to provide. Think about it: You know better than to buy a stock on one person's say-so (you do, right?) and there's a whole lot less at stake making a single stock investment than buying a home. Remember, more likely than not, your agent is paid to grease the wheels on a sale, not look after your best interests. And your friend won't lose a cent if the decision you make ends up costing you a bundle.

So before you step foot in your first open house, do yourself a favor: Conduct your own research. Not only will detailed information about the town and even the neighborhood you're considering help you choose the very best house for your investment portfolio or your family, it will also prevent you from making common home buying errors. Even if your research only brings up more questions, your informed demeanor will force agents and sellers to treat you more seriously as a buyer. In this chapter, we'll show you what data you'll need and where you can get it. We'll focus on your biggest worries—like how to tell where prices are going and whether you're likely to encounter property tax hikes. And, finally, we'll show you some pitfalls that can be easily avoided with a little homework.

Getting the Goods on Price Trends

If you've spent any time at all reading the real estate ads online or in your local newspaper, you're probably focused on just one question: How much will I have to pay to land a decent house? It's no secret why buyers are so obsessed with that single issue. Inflation-adjusted prices rose 30 percent in eight of the nation's largest metropolitan markets between 1997 and 2001, according to Harvard University's Joint Center for Housing Studies. In San Francisco, home prices soared more than 55 percent—more than double the rate of income growth in that city over the same period. Other big increases: Boston, New York, Los Angeles, Atlanta, and Washington, D.C. (See Figure 3.1 for more examples.)

What has confounded the experts is the power of the housing market even after the economy went into a tailspin. According to DataQuick Information Systems, a real estate and land data property provider based in San Diego, median home prices in the nine counties that include Silicon Valley and San Francisco were at their highest levels *ever*—$417,000—in 2002. Old-fashioned ranch-style homes traded hands for a million dollars each. And that's more than two years *after* the dot-com bust. In Denver, home prices in 2002 weren't just higher compared to 2001; they jumped nearly every month. It's not just big employment centers where housing prices have set new records. Vacation home demand is stoking record sales paces—and prices—from Michigan's lakes region to Bethany Beach in Delaware.

In fact, at its midpoint 2002 was shaping up to be another record year for price appreciation, surprising even the experts. According to mortgage lender Freddie Mac's Conventional Mortgage Home Price Index, home values grew at an annualized rate of 6.2 percent in 2002's

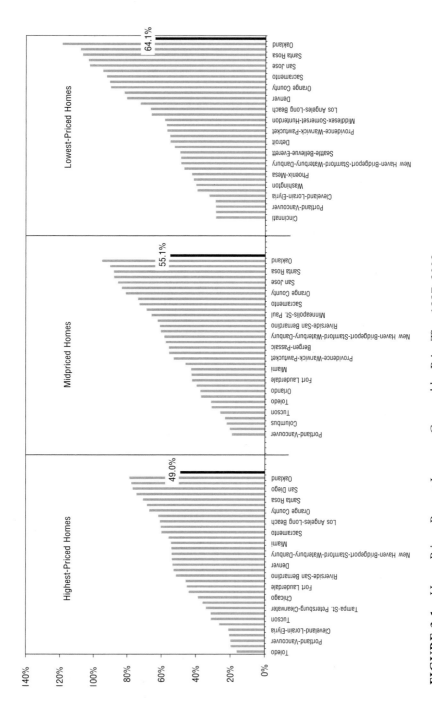

FIGURE 3.1 Home Prices, Percent Increase, Grouped by Price Tier, 1997–2002

Source: Fiserv CSW, Inc., Cambridge, Massachusetts, www.cswcasa.com.

second quarter. The leaders were Middle Atlantic states, which showed the most gains in value, growing at 9.9 percent during the second quarter, while Pacific states grew at 6.6 percent. "We haven't [previously] seen such a sustained period of national price growth," says Karl Case, a founder of the home price research firm Case Shiller Weiss and a visiting scholar at the Federal Reserve Bank of Boston. "It's been a strong market for six years."

Yet, it's becoming clear that the outsized gains can't continue, creating opportunities for investors and bargains for shoppers. For example, while San Francisco has enjoyed robust price appreciation, just 10 percent of all homes are affordable to households with median incomes, according to Harvard's housing studies center. At some point, prices will have to ease for homes to change hands. And in a surprising number of cities (think Seattle and Cleveland), price appreciation is outpacing income growth. That relationship simply can't sustain itself over time.

That fact has led to a nagging question among owners and buyers of homes: Is the red-hot housing market headed for a bust in prices just as stocks fell dramatically after a long price rise? Experts like Case concede that housing prices can stretch too far, creating an "asset bubble." But Case's own research shows that even a bust can be less worrisome to longtime homeowners than you might think. For example, Boston home prices fell 15 percent between 1989 and 1991. But homeowners who had bought their homes just five years prior to the downturn had already benefited from a 157 percent rise in prices. In other words, the bust didn't come close to touching the gains of homeowners who'd held onto their properties for several years.

The problem with the bursting of an asset bubble is what happens to people who've bought at the peak. Let's say you buy a $400,000 home, and it falls in value by 15 percent. You end up with a $340,000 home—but if you put only 10 percent down you still have $360,000 in debt. In order to sell for $340,000, you'd have to come up with $20,000 in cash to pay off your mortgage, plus an additional $20,400 if you sell using a broker. Getting trapped in such a situation can prevent you from moving for a more lucrative job or downsizing to a smaller home in a tight economy.

Rest assured, nobody is predicting a national crash in housing prices. The last time prices fell across the country—not just in one or two isolated pockets—was during the Great Depression. According to the National Association of Realtors, the average annual price gain (unadjusted for inflation) since 1968 has been 6.3 percent.

"We are not in a housing market bubble—when prices go up violating laws of supply and demand," says mortgage lender Fannie Mae chief economist David Bersen, who defines a bubble as a period in which speculators drive prices to unreasonable levels. "Today in most regions of the country demand exceeds supply. There isn't speculation."

What's more likely to happen over the next several years is that prices will rise more in line with inflation—probably about 3 percent. Only in areas that have seen the sharpest price hikes—the coasts, especially San Francisco, New York, and Boston, and a handful of cities in the interior of the country like Denver—is it likely that prices could fall. But remember, long-term holders may still come out ahead if they are able to sit tight during the downturn. And there will be regions, cities, and towns where prices rise faster than the norm over the longer term. Dallas–Fort Worth, Texas; southern California; Las Vegas; Orlando, Florida; and the Carolinas are likely to continue to prosper because of their popularity among retirees, immigrants, and foreign investors, says Mark Zandi, chief economist at Economy.com, which tracks regional economies.

To determine whether the current rise in prices you're seeing is a bubble ready to burst or simply healthy appreciation, start by checking out the single most important factor affecting housing prices: job growth. How fast your city or town creates new jobs matters because an expanding workforce translates directly into housing demand. To find out whether the job base is growing in your area, go to the federal government's Bureau of Labor Statistics web site (www.bls.gov). Click on the state and local unemployment rates, and then click again on Get Detailed Statistics on unemployment. Strong demand—job growth of 4 percent or better—portends strong housing price growth that's sustainable. Of course, you'll want to temper your outlook by checking out the supply side of the equation. Is there ample space for new homes to be built? If not, demand for homes can't be met by construction, so prices rise. (Think Manhattan.) An active new home market means that supply can expand in response to demand, keeping prices stable.

Another factor to watch: days on market. When a boom market is getting ready to cool, the first thing that happens is that it takes longer to sell the typical house because homeowners hold out for the higher price they want. Only after the days on the market statistic starts rising will you actually see prices come down. To find out how much homes have sold for in the neighborhoods you're shopping in, check the Domania web site (www.domania.com). By plugging in an address, you'll be able to get a sense of market dynamics. (Domania doesn't carry information for all states.)

Want a shortcut? Refer back to Chapter 1 for the results of our exclusive real estate forecast in Table 1.1. We weighed a variety of factors, including job growth prospects, vacancy rates, and recession resistance for 65 markets to come up with a three-year outlook.

Now that you've got a sense of prices and where they're headed, you'll want to explore more subtle issues that can impact prices or simply your peace of mind.

How Schools Affect Your Home's Value

It's common wisdom that buying a home in a superb school district acts as a sort of insurance policy on your home's value, guaranteeing steady and rising prices. Compare two similar homes, both four-bedroom split-levels built about the same time in Cincinnati, Ohio. One is located in the Wyoming school district, which is well known for its excellent schools. Asking price? $369,500. But the similar home located in Mt. Healthy's just so-so school district is priced at $155,000. It's those kinds of differences that make some people—even without children—shop neighborhoods with good schools.

If you're just moving to a new community from out of town, figuring out the Mt. Healthy and the Wyoming of your new hometown can be tough. One shortcut? High schools typically issue—for free—self-evaluations that describe students' performances on SAT scores, the number of advanced placement courses offered, and other data that will help you determine how the schools stack up. The reports are typically prepared for students to submit as part of their college admission forms, so they tend to be pretty complete. Ask the schools directly for the information, or go to the state education department's web site for details. Another source of free information: the National Association of Realtors' school report service available at its web site, Realtor.com (www.realtor.com).

But if you'd like more information (and what parent wouldn't?) check out SchoolMatch.com. The service, developed by William Bainbridge, who holds a doctorate in educational research, offers a large amount of data, ranking schools nationally using info like SAT and ACT scores and teachers' salaries. Of course, it'll cost you. SchoolMatch charges $10 for an overview of a specific school district, plus $34 for information on a school system in comparison to others in the area and nationally.

Want to conduct some of the research on your own? Bainbridge says among the most critical factors determining a school's success are the size of school district budgets, especially those dollars going to instruction, and student testing results on both college entrance exams and state and local proficiency tests. He also suggests asking the schools directly for dropout rates. Most schools are eager to supply graduation rates, he says, but most dropouts never make it to high school in the first place. Make sure, too, to ask whether the local elementary schools are accredited by the appropriate regional agencies.

One of the biggest mistakes parents make? Focusing exclusively on class size. Unless the class sizes are extremely small (12 students or less) or outsized (more than 30 students), "there's no evidence to indicate that class size makes a difference," he says.

If you don't have children and you're shopping for a home in a particularly expensive town or city, your best strategy may be to stop obsessing over picking the best district and avoiding the very worst. That's because the demographics of American families are changing. Gary Eldred, a real estate investor who served on the graduate business faculty at Stanford University, says the 2000 census showed that households containing parents with children have become a minority of the population, just 18 percent of the whole. In other words, good schools are a must for a declining proportion of the population.

How Much Will You Pay in Property Taxes?

How much tax are you going to owe on your new dream house? The short answer for most of us is plenty. Before we talk about trends, you first need to know how homes are taxed. There are two key factors to understand: the home's assessed value and your millage rate (that's the number that represents how much you owe per thousand dollars of property value). When towns want to raise taxes to support local services—the biggest piece of which are usually schools—they can either change the millage rate or reassess properties. The big trend among tax collectors is to increase the frequency with which home values are reassessed. In Kansas, for example, homes are reassessed every year; in Missouri it's every other year. That makes it critical that you make a quick trip to the local town hall's tax assessor's office to find out if any changes are pending.

Now, if you are moving to a neighborhood where prices have been increasing handily, beware: Your local government wants a piece of the action. There are two reasons that local governments increasingly have their hands in homeowners' pockets: First off, the reduction of federal government spending for services that began under President Ronald Reagan has shifted responsibility to states and local governments. Second, the recession has only increased the need for local governments to prime the pump with property tax revenues. "The 1990s was an era when everything was increasing. There was a shift of services to the states, which could easily be absorbed then, but with the economic downturn it's more difficult," says Paul Welcome, president of the International Association of Assessing Officers.

Having big industry in your town may be no guarantee of low taxes, either. Becky Fagg, a Lexington, South Carolina, grandmother who is leading a no-tax movement in her home state, says that there's another factor that is raising homeowners' tax bills: the economic development packages bestowed on companies by local governments eager to increase their tax bases. These incentives generally mean low or no property taxes assessed to the business. Who makes it up? Individual property owners. "Anytime you give an exemption, you're shifting the burden to someone else," says Welcome.

Fagg has endured property tax increases of 180 percent even as companies like Pirelli and Michelin moved to her county. She became so angry over the years due to repeated tax hikes that she's led a movement that ousted county administrators opposed to lowering taxes and even started shaking up state government officials.

Of course, if you have some flexibility in the location of your new home, you'll want to choose low-tax towns. Buyers of second homes or vacation homes should make sure that they aren't buying in a rural region that's actually losing population. Sooner or later the local government officials will have to raise your tax bill to make up for the loss in tax revenues. Keep in mind, too, says Welcome, that if you've got your heart set on living in a specific school district, the cities feeding into those school districts may well have very different millage rates. For example, children in the cities of Overland Park and Leawood, Kansas, can choose the same school districts. Yet Leawood's millage rate of 21.815 is nearly three times higher than Overland Park's 7.649 rate.

Neighbor versus Neighbor

Locating neighborhoods that have both good schools and low taxes is key to finding the house of your dreams. But your research shouldn't stop there. That's because there are other issues that can affect how happy you'll be in your new home—and perhaps even the value of your property.

One of the big issues roiling neighborhoods where property values have soared is teardowns. In neighborhoods where the price of land typically exceeds that of the home sitting on it, buyers are tearing down charming Cape Cod cottages and claustrophobic ranches, and building larger homes that push the boundaries of their properties. Neighbors angered by changes in their neighborhoods' aesthetics sometimes seek regulatory changes to prevent the conversions.

When *SmartMoney* first wrote about the phenomenon in 1999, we focused on a small suburb of Chicago called Hinsdale, Illinois. There, some 15 percent of the housing stock was being torn down and re-built—considerably more than the trend nationally. (The National Association of HomeBuilders has said about 10 percent of the homes built are teardowns.) If you're unwittingly buying into such an area with no plans to upgrade, you may find yourself in the middle of a war zone.

In Hinsdale, renovators exercising what they felt were their rights as property owners found themselves besieged by neighbors' complaints. Longtime owners complained about views obstructed by bigger homes, and the constant construction disruptions. They said the aesthetics of their town were being destroyed. The conflict played out at village trustee meetings and over backyard fences as neighbors squared off against their neighbors. One middle-aged woman was arrested for reckless conduct after driving her Mercedes through the still-wet concrete driveway of a teardown neighbor. Imagine yourself moving to such a neighborhood: It's not exactly the kind of community environment that promotes the peace and tranquility you may be seeking for your family. But it'd be hard to miss all the bulldozers and tractors a teardown-prone neighborhood invariably attracts.

If teardowns wreck your sanity, however, suburban sprawl may be more costly.

Northern Virginia's fantastic growth of the past decade may have benefited longtime property owners who were able to take advantage of rising prices. But families who moved to the region in recent years have found themselves ensnarled in traffic, fighting for basic services. In Loudoun County, for example, the population doubled to 300,000 during the 1990s. Chris Miller is president of the Piedmont Environmental Council, the group that effectively lobbied against Disney's proposed construction of a theme park in nearby Prince William County. He says that the region's rapid-fire growth can't be sustained by taxpayers. "Loudoun is spread out over a 150,000-acre area, and the cost of providing services is crippling them. They have to build 40 schools in the next decade."

The prospect of not getting one of those schools reasonably close to her South Riding village neighborhood has transformed Barbara Munsey, a mother of two, into a self-described "public pitbull." When she first moved to the area, which had been farmland, her children weren't yet in school. After school construction plans were delayed twice, Munsey started routinely attending every meeting of county administrators, the school board, anywhere she might have an opportunity to push her cause. Now that her kids are aged 8 and 6, Munsey is engaged in a battle of words with neighbors in Brambleton over who will get the school first. The county recently promised to push both projects, but Munsey figures it's unlikely that both will get built.

In her fight, she's endured insults. People decried the rampant development of Loudoun, likening growth to a cancer. "We are a cancer! Can you imagine? They are talking about *me*." And that wasn't the worst that happened. One Brambleton mother even accused Munsey of stalking her after Munsey correctly deduced that the woman lived doors away from the ringleader of the Brambleton movement.

For all the warring, however, Munsey is no closer to getting the high school the county originally promised residents would open in 2003. In fact, it looks like Brambleton may end up getting its school first, and South Riding children will have to take a long bus trip to and from classes and after-school activities.

Could Loudoun's trouble been foreseen? Possibly. Areas that have endured rapid-fire development routinely encounter trouble paying up for the required infrastructure—streets, services, and schools. At the very least, the chances of encountering rising property tax bills are high. If you're moving to such an area, you'll want to get a good handle on the local political scene as well as the ability of local government to pay for services. One way to do that is to check out the local government's bond ratings. Services like Standard & Poor's and Moody's Investors Service assign grades to the debt issued by municipalities, which you can check out at their web sites. A grade of AAA is the best. Junk status of B or lower means you may find yourself facing higher taxes.

Three-Headed Rabbits

Bill Studenc was just about to break ground on his dream house in Waynesville, North Carolina, several years ago, when the local government let fly some devastating news at a public meeting. Water from a well serving a house in the same subdivision had just tested positive for arsenic and lead. Previous owners of the mountainside property had operated an apple orchard on the site, and for decades the trees had been sprayed with a combination of lead and arsenic thought to be lethal only to the bugs that might destroy the apple crop. It turns out, though, that exposure to such elements over time poses health hazards to humans, too. Studenc and his wife, Margaret, had just sold their cramped house, and were looking forward to moving to the up-scale neighborhood in which yards were separated by stone fences and well-tended gardens dotted the landscape.

"I said, 'What have I done? I've sold the house out from under my family, and we don't have anyplace else to go,' " recalls Studenc, associate director of public information at Western Carolina University. "It was probably the single most stressful period of our lives."

More troubling is the fact that Studenc had heard talk of problems at the site—what he called "three-headed rabbit rumors"—and had even tried to investigate by questioning county and state health department officials. They reassured him that water tests at the site had never shown any sign of bacterial contamination. Later, when a representative of the state health department said publicly that the chances of getting sick from the water in the subdivision were one in a million, it laid to rest all of Studenc's fears.

Then came the public meeting. What Studenc heard stunned him. The reason the health officials hadn't believed there was a problem was because they'd never tested for arsenic and lead. Regulatory guidelines require testing for only bacterial contamination, not for pesticides. The crowd of about 200 at the public meeting met the news with disbelief, then anger. "We had been told it was safe," says Studenc, recalling the reaction in the room. "How can you tell us it's not safe? Who can we sue?"

For a year the couple was in limbo as they waited for the findings at the one property to be affirmed throughout the subdivision. Some neighbors talked about a group lawsuit, but the effort went nowhere. Luckily, his contractor accepted the fact he wanted to wait. After further testing, the Environmental Protection Agency (EPA) told the Studencs that while they could go ahead and build their house, it would be unsafe to drink water from a well on the property. What's more, the EPA advised against allowing the children to play in the yard. Studenc remembers thinking, "What kind of home is that?" Eventually, the subdivision became a Superfund site, and the EPA stepped in to clean up the problem. But there was another catch-22 for the couple. The agency removed topsoil from lots with houses, but refused to clean the Studencs' property. Since it was empty, the EPA rationale went, there was no threat to human health.

In the end, Studenc figures he got lucky. His contractor allowed him to walk away from his contract to build the home, and he was able to sell the land at a small profit after the area was promised a public water supply. But he knows that had the market been softer, he might never have been able to unload the property.

What can you do to make sure you don't end up with that kind of problem? Matthew Wilson, director at Toxics Action Center, a nonprofit organization that tracks polluted sites, says many states have databases online that track existing toxic waste sites—not former apple orchards, but a range of sites from incinerators to radioactive waste. That'll help you stay away from hazards that are already well known, but if you're concerned that perhaps your bucolic new neighborhood used to be an orchard like the Studencs', Wilson suggests checking insurance maps known as Sanborn maps at your local library that detail previous usage. He also suggests interviewing neighbors to find out about any "three-headed rabbit rumors." Finally, if you're worried about groundwater contamination, a standard water test called an Phase 1 ATM will run you $2,000 to $3,000, which is not a big investment if what you're buying is peace of mind.

In sum, when you're investigating a town or city, you'll want to understand intimately just where prices are likely to head, whether taxes are rising or falling, and what school districts can contribute to your home's value. Don't forget to check more subtle issues that can affect prices and your ability to sleep at night. We'll use all this information in the next chapter to zero in on the right property.

4

Zeroing In on the Right Property

With any luck at all, you've now narrowed your search to just one town or neighborhood, and have eliminated the areas with poor schools or high taxes. You've even learned to pick up on more subtle issues—like entrenched neighborhood squabbles and overdevelopment—that could affect your happiness after your purchase. In this chapter, we'll rev up your search to warp speed, helping you figure out whether the neighborhood you've chosen is experiencing a buyer's or a seller's market; and we'll give you buying strategies for each. We'll also expose the telltale clues that owners leave behind at open houses that will give you an edge in negotiating for your dream house.

If you're buying a house or other property as an investment, this chapter will guide you through the next level of decision making. What kind of property is right for you? What investing strategy makes sense? The answers are just ahead.

Strategies for Home Buyers

After reading the previous chapter, you may feel you've got a pretty good handle on prices in the town you're targeting. But as any experienced real estate investor can tell you, even within markets, price trends can vary—and dramatically. Consider this: When prices stalled briefly in early 2000 in San Francisco Bay area, it was the luxury market where prices were most dramatically affected. While owners of the most expensive homes were forced to knock 20 and even 30 percent off the prices they were asking for their properties, prices for starter homes were still rising.

For that reason, relying on median prices released by your local real estate association isn't going to tell you much about the trends that matter most to you. A better way to get detailed local information is to conduct an informal survey of prices on homes that are comparable to what you'd like to buy. Start by going to the web site for the National Association of Realtors (www.realtor.com), which has the most comprehensive home listings in the country. Search the site for homes with exactly the parameters you're looking for, including number of bedrooms and baths and square footage, in the area you are targeting. If you're dead set on a pool or other special items, include them, too. Now, divide the purchase price of each home by the square footage to come up with a price per square foot. The result is a number you can use to compare one property to another. When you start touring homes, do the calculation on these properties as well. After making several comparisons, you'll start to get a clear idea of what you can expect to pay for your dream home. You'll know when homes are overpriced and when they are underpriced.

Since asking and sales prices tend to diverge when markets are in flux, get your agent to put together a list of recent sales prices of comparable houses in the area. Then ask to be kept as up-to-date as possible on what homes are selling for in the area or at least how close the sales prices are to the asking prices. (Even though the information won't be made public for weeks, agents usually have a pretty clear idea of how much homes are actually selling for.)

One other piece of information is key: days on market—the number of days a home takes to sell, from listing to contract. Changes in this number will clue you in to big-time market moves. If the number is rising, prices will fall. Likewise, if the amount of time it takes to sell properties is getting shorter, prices may be ready to spike. Compare these numbers to the long-term averages. One caution: Real estate markets don't turn on a dime. If sellers fear they won't be able to get the prices they want out of their homes, they are normally loath to put them on the market.

While you're searching, continue to pay attention to any big layoff announcements from local companies that will impact demand in the area where you want to buy. When Mel Schmidt was bidding for his house in Austin, Texas, he was stunned at the stratospheric prices sellers were demanding while the local economy appeared fragile. The seller refused to budge from the $215,000 asking price, and Schmidt felt he'd be paying too much. Negotiations stalled. Then news broke that Motorola, the city's fourth-largest employer, was cutting 4,000 jobs. Schmidt told the seller's broker to take a look at the headlines in the local paper. "This was my notice to their client to wake up and smell the coffee," he says. Schmidt offered $209,500. "Within five minutes they accepted my offer."

Where to Look

Now that you're armed with detailed information about the local market, you're ready to exploit current conditions. If you're targeting one of those areas where prices are falling, you'll have the luxury of extending your search to homes priced above your target range. Homes most likely to come down in price are those that have been on the market a month or more. When sellers hire an agent to sell their house they usually sign a listing contract that gives the agent 90 days to sell the house. Remember, the closer the broker is to the end of the contract the more likely he or she is to push the seller to accept any offer. Be patient, though, counsels Curtis Hall, a RE/MAX agent in Tempe, Arizona. "When the market shifts, it takes a little while for everyone to figure it out," he says.

When prices begin to slip in your area, target the smaller pockets where they'll drop first and furthest. Chris Sargeant, a district sales manager for a networking company in San Francisco, started looking for a house in 2000, when prices were rising 28 percent over the year before. "The market was full of paper millionaires, and people placing ridiculous bids," he recalls. Disappointed, he dropped out for a while.

In the fall, though, his business orders started tapering off. "The Internet community was running out of money," he says. So Sargeant looked at lofts in the South of Market area, which had been favored by dot-com workers. After two months, he landed a loft for $50,000 less than the asking price of $599,000.

Another way to maximize your leverage is by finding spec homes. These new houses, built "on speculation"—without buyers lined up first—are sometimes the first to experience price reductions. One quick way to figure out whether any of these spec homes are in your neighborhood is by pointing your browser to eBay (www.ebay.com), which is auctioning homes from builders across the country like KB Home and Beazer Homes.

If, however, you're in one of those markets where prices are continuing to climb, you may want to consider expanding your search to include neighborhoods that other buyers have overlooked. In Boston, for example, buyers set on looking in fashionable, but expensive, Back Bay might opt for the South End, a close-by neighborhood similarly stocked with restaurants and trendy shops, but one where prices are more reasonable because the neighborhood isn't as established as the Back Bay. Likewise, buyers attracted to San Francisco's pricey Noe Valley, a neighborhood popular with young engineers commuting to Silicon Valley, might opt instead to look in nearby Glen Park, where prices aren't as steep.

The problem with remaining inflexible on neighborhood, says B. J. Droubi, a real estate broker whose agency specializes in Noe Valley properties, is that it's all too easy to get drawn into a bidding war in red-hot neighborhoods. If that's the case, she says, "set your limit and don't go over it."

One woman who didn't set such limits now regrets it. The

How to Find a Well Cared For Home

The first time you traipse through an open house, you may be so distracted by the owner's taste in furnishings—*purple leather couches? harvest gold kitchen appliances? shag carpeting?*—that you can barely bring yourself to look at the really important stuff. And if you're new to the process of buying for investment or for your own use, you many not even know what to watch for. Let's face it, not too many of us have backgrounds in architecture or engineering. Real estate agents like to talk about "good bones," when a home's basic design and structure are sound and pleasing to the eye, and they're happy to tell you when *they* think a property is a winner, but wouldn't it be great if you could figure it out yourself?

Ron Hazelton has some answers. The host of the television show *HouseCalls*, Hazelton has made a career of examining the interiors of hundreds of homes across the country, helping people with improvement projects large and small. Because of his experience, he's in a unique position to explain how you can tell which home has been well taken care of—and is therefore a good

Ron Hazelton

candidate to buy—and which one's slapdash paint job is covering some sort of horror that will have you borrowing money from your 401(k) to set straight.

So where does he start? One of his favorite places is the basement. The main thing he looks for there is signs of water damage or seepage—the number one enemy of a home's foundation. If the owner has sump pumps feverishly cranking out the water, watch out. One common warning sign: a white powdery substance showing up on basement walls. What that indicates is that water pressure is building up on the outside of the walls underground, pushing minerals, called efflorescence, through the basement walls. Usually this problem can be treated pretty easily by painting the walls with a sealant. But if it's really serious, the remedies are far more radical and expensive—and could entail digging up the exterior around your home to install a curtain or french drain.

Water's not the only issue for basements. You also want to make sure that the house isn't settling in a way that would make the foundation buckle or strain. Keep your eyes peeled for any cracks in basement walls that run on the diagonal. They signal a potential settlement or movement problem. Similarly, look out for cracks between the basement floor and the wall, which indicate a separation between the slab that the house sits on and the basement walls.

You'll want to be just as careful checking out the house's roof and siding or exterior. "They're big-ticket items to repair," Hazelton says. Start by crawling up into the attic. "I'd be looking at the underside of the roof. Is there any distortion in the rafters? Is the roof warping? [That] could indicate several layers of roofing, and once you've got three layers you can't add any more," he says. A home inspector can help you figure out whether a roof has inadequate ventilation or insulation. Either can be a problem. A roof that doesn't allow heat to escape can create ice damming in the winter, while a roof that isn't adequately insulated will cost you a fortune in heating bills.

When you're done with the roof, check out the exterior finish of the house. If it is clear the house hasn't been painted in a long time, look for damaged or weathered shingles or siding. While such deterioration is typically a slow process, the potential costs are high. Who wants to pay to re-side a house? In fact, Hazelton is so wary of siding issues he even inspects new paint jobs just to make sure they aren't hiding a weather damage problem. As long as you're outside the home, you'll also want to poke around the shubbery next to the house to make sure that you don't see any mud tunnels that are evidence of termites.

Inside the house, you'll want to give the plumbing the once-over. The best pipes are copper, but plastic is quite common and a sturdy replacement. Steel pipes can collect minerals in areas where water has a high mineral content, restricting capacity. Hazelton says as he tours a house he'll turn on all the water spigots in the bathrooms at the same time (and flush the toilet) to make sure the water pressure is good. Banging pipes are a bad sign; watch for any evidence of leaks in cabinets under sinks.

When it comes to the electrical system, you'll rely for the most part on your inspector, but you can at least count the number of circuit breakers. Hazelton says the more the better, with a dozen or even 20 adequate for the average home.

That's a short tour of some of issues you'll want to watch for when looking at potential homes to buy. Hazelton offers one other piece of advice: Neatness counts. If you enter a home where the closets are orderly, the attic neat, and even the cabinets below the sink organized, chances are better than even that the home has been well looked after.

"When I look at a house, I open up closets. I'm trying to determine whether the house has been quickly put up for sale or it's been taken care of all along. If clothes and shoes and boxes are jammed in, that's a bad sign. I can look beyond some of this stuff, but I prefer a house that's been taken care of. It says this family has been a custodian of the house and they haven't let problems accumulate, and I can have confidence in this house."

woman, a client of Droubi's, won a bidding war for a San Francisco house put on the market two years ago at $875,000. Her $1.2 million bid trumped 12 others. But when she tried to sell, none of the offers she drew covered what she still owed on the house. She was forced to negotiate with her bankers for a "short sale." In other words, her bank would agree to accept an offer below the value of the mortgage and write off the difference. A caveat: A short sale, while better than defaulting on your mortgage, creates other problems. You'll face income taxes on the difference between the value of your mortgage and the sale price of the house. A short sale is a last resort. If you can hold your property off the market until prices recover, do so.

Regardless of whether you're in a buyer's or seller's market, once you start looking at homes you'll want to keep your eyes peeled for obvious clues that sellers leave behind that can give you valuable leverage in a negotiation. "We try to find out what's going on in the sellers' lives," says RE/MAX's Hall. "I look for the clues—the little crumbs that Hansel and Gretel leave along the way."

Depressions in the carpet where furniture used to be and half-empty master bedroom closets signal that the couple who own the house, are seeking a divorce and may want to move quickly. Boxes from a national moving company signal a corporate relocation—and anxious sellers. And if you find For Sale by Owner signs in the garage or For Sale signs from a brokerage other than the one you're dealing with, the owners may be feeling a little desperate. In each of these cases, your ability to ensure a quick and smooth close could net you a better price.

When a buyer really gets serious about a particular property, Hall likes to check with the local title company to find out whether there are any liens or second mortgages on the property. This will often give him clues about how long the owners have held the mortgage and how much they continue to owe on the property, as well as whether the owners are under any financial pressures. And that kind of information will help you figure how to negotiate the right price.

How to Negotiate

Once you've found your castle, here's the key to negotiating price in markets where prices have stalled, or, better yet, have fallen: Slow down. Most people want to rush the negotiations, especially buyers in red-hot markets who've grown accustomed to having to compete with multiple bidders. No doubt your broker and lawyer will also try to hurry you, since they get paid after you sign on the dotted line. But if the market is moving in your favor, "no one should fool you into believing there's not another house around the corner," says Bradley Inman, founder of HomeGain.com, a web site that connects buyers with real estate agents. "You can take your time."

Tara and Rick Ray used this technique to good effect when buying their home near Kansas City, Missouri. The two, financial planners who were relocating from Minneapolis, found a gem of a house alongside an 18-hole golf course. The Rays saw big savings in choosing the location—their two children could attend public school, eliminating the $10,000 annual private school tuition they'd been paying. In addition, they'd get reduced golf memberships. During the two months the couple spent looking in the area, the price on the house dropped to $949,000 from $999,000 as the high-end market weakened. The Rays offered a lowball $875,000. "It was our first choice, but sometimes you've got to take some risks," Rick says. It worked. The owners countered with $939,000. The Rays then took a couple of days to chew on the counter, netting another $10,000 price reduction.

If you can't wrangle a concession on price, remember that you can negotiate any element of the deal. When Carter and Holly Davis were bidding on a home in the suburbs between Dallas and Fort Worth in 2001, they offered the full asking price. But they requested that the owner pay their $3,000 closing costs. He complied, and the deal was done.

It's not everyone who's going to have the luxury of negotiating for a home in the middle of a buyer's market. In fact, because home prices

What to Look For in a Home Inspector

When Dian Gilmore first saw the recently renovated brick home in one of Phoenix's historic neighborhoods, she couldn't conceal her excitement.

The house had the magic combination of size and price she had been looking for. Its three bedrooms and two baths fit her needs perfectly, and its $152,000 price tag was well within her budget. "It looked wonderful," she recalls. "It had a nicely landscaped yard, flowers in the flower box. Nothing looked out of place."

But the house's neat-as-a-pin exterior masked fundamental problems, as Gilmore found once she hired a housing inspector to take a look at the property. In a five-hour marathon inspection, she learned that the house she was about to buy had a roof that was damaged and leaking. The dishwasher line wasn't hooked up. Air-conditioning ducts passed through the fireplace flue, creating a fire hazard. To top it off, a six-foot grounding rod for the home's electrical system had been driven right through the sewer line, which would have caused the toilets to eventually back up and waste to collect underneath her house.

"The family had done the renovation themselves and cut every corner," she says. "It upset me to think I was going to put 20 percent down, and it would have been my biggest investment."

Gilmore promptly backed out of the deal and a month later found a home that passed its inspection with flying colors. "When I think about how much money I saved by not buying that house, I am still grateful," she says. "I averted the *Titanic*."

As Gilmore's experience shows, a good housing inspection can save you no end of headaches. But getting a good inspector isn't easy. Max Gordon, a real estate agent in Overland Park, Kansas, warns that some inspectors get too close to the agents who recommend them, failing to represent the buyers adequately in order to make sure they get more business. "It doesn't happen that often, but with some inspectors there may be a question of where there loyalty lies," he says.

Some real estate agents simply recommend the inspector who works the most quickly. That's good for the agent, who's interested in closing the deal, but bad if you want the home closely inspected. Don't expect much help from state agencies in finding a competent inspector, either, since relatively few states license inspectors or test them. In fact, in some states manicurists are more heavily regulated than house inspectors.

To find a reliable professional, then, don't just take the first name your agent gives you. Start by checking out the web site of the American Society of Home Inspectors (ASHI) at www.ashi.org. Once there, you'll find a search engine for members of the group, each of whom is required to have conducted at least 250 paid inspections. Prior experience matters; there's little in the way of training programs for these professionals.

But don't stop your investigation there. To narrow down that list, ask potential candidates how many years they've been working as inspectors, and what their backgrounds were before they started inspecting homes. Make sure you understand exactly what parts of the house your inspector will look at, and which he or she won't. Some don't do tests you may find critical. You may have to hire someone else (and pay more) to test for mold, air quality, and radon. Ask for references that you can call, and even ask to see a sample inspection report. A good inspector will have patience with your questions.

A warning signal that you've got a bad inspector: He tells you he knows someone who can make the repairs necessary to the leaky roof you're about to buy. Offering services is a no-no, says ASHI's executive director Rob Paterkiewicz. "He's supposed to be an independent and objective third party," he says. That means no ties to realtors or remodelers.

Once you hire your inspector, make sure you attend the inspection and ask questions along the way. A good review of an average-sized house will take two to three hours. It's important you stay engaged because inspectors are required to look only for major defects—electricity that's not grounded, air-conditioning or heating systems that are operating in an unsafe manner. If you

SIDEBAR 4.2

want them to go further, you'll have to prod them yourself. Some will take digital photographs of the roof and other difficult-to-reach places so that you can see them for yourself.

Don't think you can skip an inspection if you're buying a new home. Max Gordon once insisted a new home be inspected over the selling agent's wishes; it was found that the flue going from the furnace to the chimney had come apart at the seam and would've vented carbon monoxide throughout the house. The best thing to do if you're buying a new home is to have it inspected even before the finishing touches are put on, he says. That way your inspector can check out the foundations, framing, and drainage as the house is being built.

The average cost for a home inspection nationally, according to ASHI, is $300. But as Gilmore can tell you, it can be money well spent.

tend to move slowly but consistently higher, you're much more likely to be making an offer when it seems that sellers have every advantage. In those cases, you'll want to use every tool at your disposal—sniffing out the clues that can help you gain some leverage and finding the owners' weak spots.

That's what Jay and Marianne Dean did when they were desperately trying to find a new home for their family of four smack-dab in the middle of the go-go housing market in northern California. Each Saturday, Marianne would rise at 6 A.M., scoop up the *Palo Alto Weekly*, and jump in the car to check the houses in the real estate ads before the kids got up. On Sundays, the whole family would pile into the car to go to the open houses, one spouse watching the kids while the other gave the potential prizes the once-over.

But they couldn't seem to buy a home. They bid on three houses and lost out on all three—their offer on one ranch got crushed by a rival bid $200,000 higher.

Then in January, Marianne discovered that a 2,800-square-foot ranch house in Redwood City they had seen five weeks earlier was still on the market. Five weeks—it was ancient by northern California standards. What's more, they knew there was nothing wrong with the house except maybe the price.

Sensing opportunity, the two got on the phone with their agent, pushing her to call the seller's agent immediately. What they learned was golden: The owners were retiring to Florida, and if they didn't sell soon they'd face financing their retirement with an expensive bridge loan.

Jay Dean offered $150,000 less than the owner's $1.35 million asking price and promised to close quickly. He'd already gotten his mortgage prequalified and they had waived the customary house inspection. "We wanted their worries to go away," says Jay. Six hours later the owners caved in and the Deans grabbed the house for $1.225 million. "You have to be ready," he says. "So if any opportunity presents itself, you can jump on it."

Options for Real Estate Investors

If you're buying a home for a family, your choices are pretty much limited to single-family homes and condominiums. But if you want to invest in real estate, the options are numerous—and confusing to the newcomer. Raw land or apartment buildings? Should you flip properties, buying a house one week and selling it the next? Maybe you want to buy the office building that houses your business.

Here's a brief overview of the range of properties you might consider investing in.

Land

What could be better than investing in the raw material of real estate, land? The savvy investor who manages to snap up property right in front of a wave of development can score big. But while the potential payoff is large, the risks also are huge. Let's face it, that wave of development you're betting on could grind to a halt if the economy turns sour. Don't forget, too, that most land speculators improve their properties, spending hours before county planning commissions and zoning panels getting parcels that were once zoned for agricultural uses upgraded to prime industrial or residential. But that's not all. Owners may also bring utilities to a site, grade the land so it can easily be developed, or even landscape some portions of it. Plus, unlike a rental property, you'll have no income to offset the carrying costs—taxes and interest—of your property, or to fund the upgrades. Investing in land is a highly speculative game best left to experts, especially on a large scale. However, smaller pieces of land, particularly those in the middle of large developments, can be particularly attractive and may require less work.

Office Buildings

There are plenty of choices in this category: Small single-tenant buildings and multitenant buildings in office or industrial parks are examples. Watch out for properties dominated by just one or two tenants since turnover could cost you a bundle if you were unable to replace them right away. And make sure you understand the local business climate and how it's driving rents, which tend to run in cycles. A good commercial office broker may be your best guide to this market. Although long-term leases are a real attraction to investing in office space (most businesses sign up for at least five years), remember that each time a tenant turns over you may have to change the entire layout of the space for a new tenant.

Buying office space makes the most sense for professionals and entrepreneurs who are faced with paying for their own office space. But here we're talking about a small two- or three-tenant building, not Rockefeller Center. Lawyers and doctors, in particular, can benefit from buying a small office building, using a portion of the square footage, and leasing the rest. Robert Hockett, an Atlanta financial adviser, advises his doctor clients to sell the building when they sell their practice.

Retail

For most of us, multimillion-dollar regional mall development is out of the question. Leave that to the Rouses and Mel Simons of the world. The same goes for the power centers, developments that claim several discount retailers, like Wal-Mart and Home Depot, as tenants. But plenty of small investors buy strip centers or neighborhood retail centers. (What's the difference between these? Strip malls are small, with 5,000 to 25,000 square feet of space, while strip centers are far larger and tend to be located where several residential neighborhoods converge.)

A typical stumbling block for investors in these properties is keeping the right mix of tenants on hand. In addition, managing one of these properties can be a full-time job that has more than a few frustrations. Jay Butler, director of the Arizona Real Estate Center at Arizona State University, says one retail tenant of a strip mall he owned got so angry with him once that he paid his rent in nickels. "Managing these suckers can be a headache," he says.

Apartment Buildings

Maybe you're looking at rental rates in your area and thinking, "Why settle for one lease when I can get rental payments from two, three, or twenty?" In other words, why not buy an entire apartment building or a large residence you can rent to several families?

But apartment buildings are one of the most popular investments for another reason altogether: They claim the best tax treatment on depreciation of all investments. Owners can write off the cost of the building over 27 and a half years. That may not sound like much, but if you are buying and holding a property for the long term it's a solid tax break.

Apartments, though, have their own headaches. The first is this: Unless you own more than 50 units, you'll have difficulty finding professionals to manage the building, says Butler. And if you're thinking of living on-site, you'll have to be prepared for the any-hour-of-the-day calls likely to come from tenants. Apartment buildings can be good investments, but are best bought once you have a little experience under your belt.

Rental Homes

Far and away the most common way individual investors get into real estate is with an individual home they plan to rent out. Investing in a rental home plays to small investors' strengths: You probably already have had the experience of buying and managing your own home. What's more, if you've lived in your community for any period at all you have a good sense of what neighborhoods are attractive, where the good schools are, and where most of the employers are. All of those things can help you decide where to buy.

Tim Hayes used his knowledge of Rochester, New York, where he has lived all his life, to pick a neighborhood where he's likely to purchase. He chose a section of town called "White Pants Alley" after the scrubs worn by doctors and researchers who populate the area around the University of Rochester's research hospital. Hayes, whose wife is a doctor, figures that medical professionals "aren't going to trash the place. They don't move out every six months." A lot of the time they aren't even home because of the demands of residency. Hayes's strategy will be to hold his rental properties for 20 years, paying down the mortgages all the while. By the time he retires, he figures his rents will provide a significant portion of his retirement income.

But buying a home that you turn into a successful rental demands that you amply cover your costs—your mortgage, taxes, and upkeep—with monthly rent, what the experts call "cash flow positive." "In some areas, it's extremely difficult to get started in rental housing because you can't get rent to cover your mortgage," real estate investor Gary Eldred says. "You have to tailor your investment strategy to your area."

How do you do that? Start by combing your local newspaper to get a sense of rental rates for the size home you intend to buy. Next, see whether your carrying costs can be covered by those rents. Use the mortgage calculator at www.smartmoney.com to help you determine you monthly mortgage payment for an average-priced house in your neighborhood. Then, add together the monthly mortgage, monthly taxes (a real estate agent can help with this), and upkeep costs, including insurance, maintenance, repairs, and any other outlays you'll likely encounter on an ongoing basis. If average rents in the area don't come close to covering your fixed costs, you may want to consider other ways of investing in real estate.

For example, a $125,000 home bought for 20 percent down might require a monthly mortgage payment of about $650. Given taxes of $600 a month, insurance costs of $35, and maintenance of $100, rental income would have to be nearly $1,400 to cover fixed costs. Most investors like to see a large cushion over and above the mortgage to fund major repairs and provide a profit.

Strategies for Real Estate Investors

You don't have to go any further than your living room to find advice on investing strategies. Tune in to late-night television and you're almost certain to find an infomercial on the wonders of "flipping" properties or "nothing down" real estate investing. Venturing out to your neighborhood bookstore, you'll find plenty of books that promise to turn you into a millionaire on your first deal. Does this sound a little bit like dot-com investing several years ago? No doubt. Most savvy real estate investors, though, aren't looking for the quick buck, but rather a consistent moneymaking machine that can keep pumping profits into their retirement. Choose your strategy carefully for making consistent profits in real estate.

Renting Out Single-Family Homes

More than any other strategy, individuals who invest in homes with the purpose of renting them out seem to have consistent success, especially when it comes to first-time investors. That's mainly because, as we said before, investors have more experience buying single-family homes in the first place.

If you're buying a home for investment, rather than to live in, keep in mind these things: First off, avoid a home with a distinctive style or expensive finishing touches. Remember, your tastes and your tenants' tastes may be completely different. Tenants may not take care of that fancy tile work in the kitchen that you paid extra for. Most rental homes are in moderate-income neighborhoods, but you'll find plenty of rental homes in wealthy neighborhoods as well, because the long period of rising housing prices has locked some potential first-time buyers out of the market.

Wendy Weinstein, a consumer marketing consultant in Larchmont, New York, got her start as a landlord after inheriting her grandmother's home in an upscale neighborhood. Weinstein's is a classic Westchester County suburb, populated with commuters to Wall Street and midtown Manhattan. Yet because her neighborhood is also close to a French school that draws the children of European executives temporarily assigned to the United States, Weinstein figured she might have the opportunity to rent the house out and hold on to the property. It has worked like a charm. She rents the house long-term, recently signing a four-year contract for $290,000, nearly $6,000 a month. She gets tenants directly from the school itself or through an agent who works with the 50 new families who come to the town each year.

The Perils of Flipping Homes

Flipping homes generally means buying properties and quickly reselling them to others, earning tens of thousands of dollars for each flip (at least that's the dream). The practice became popular during the late 1990s, when low interest rates and a burgeoning class of investors interested in developing their own real estate businesses started forming investment clubs all over the country. Often they flipped the properties to each other.

One of the true believers was Andy Schlotterbeck, whom *Smart-Money* first interviewed back in 1998. He was so adept at buying and selling homes quickly that friends in his investing club in Cincinnati had taken to calling him the Flipping King. Today he's still investing, but his strategy has changed—pretty dramatically. "In the beginning, I would find a good deal and sell it to another buyer," he says. "I'd tie it up with a 30-day contract, talk it up to investors, and I'd sell it to them for just a little more money. That's a good way to start," he says. "But the real wealth comes from buying and holding."

In fact, today's flippers risk trouble in a market where prices aren't always marching steadily higher. "You can get whipsawed, as many people did in the early 1990s when people were renovating in the upswing and tried to sell in the downturn," says real estate investor Gary Eldred. "Flipping presumes a rising market—you have to be very careful about how much money you're putting into the property."

Some investors—call them serial renovators—flip but make much of their profit on the sweat equity they put into the homes they improve. Harlan Furbush's full-time job is as a RE/MAX real estate agent in Rochester, New York, but his hobby is renovating homes, using the proceeds to fund his retirement account. "It's a lot like buying stocks—you need to know the numbers," he says. "I may look at 30 homes before I choose one."

In a typical deal, like the one he finished recently, he bought a rundown property in a working-class neighborhood for $27,500 from the bank that had foreclosed on it. Vacant for two years, the house was a crumbling disaster. His first move was to mow the overgrown lawn; then he removed a dilapidated garage using chain saws and a Dumpster. Over the next seven months, he and his partner, a handyman with technical skills, refurbished the bathroom and kitchen, rewired the house, replaced the plumbing, put in hardwood floors, and painted the interior. When he and his partner sold the house, it brought $63,000, the second highest sales price on the street in several years.

"To me, it's therapy," he says.

Being successful at renovating and reselling takes technical skill and savvy about neighborhoods, plus tons of time. Furbush typically spends 5 A.M. to noon each Tuesday and Thursday and the occasional Friday or Saturday night on properties he's renovating.

His risk, as with all people who turn properties around in a relatively short time, is that in the interim prices could fall, reducing or even removing his profit.

The Attraction of Syndication

If all this sounds like way too much work (and we haven't even started talking about what it takes to be a landlord yet), you might consider investing in a syndicated real estate deal, sometimes called a limited partnership. Syndicating a deal simply means bringing together investors (who might not otherwise know each other) to invest together, in this case in a real estate project. Typically, a real estate broker, a developer, or anyone else with real estate experience (the general partner) puts together a deal and explains in a disclosure statement the expected returns and the possible pitfalls. The deals can underwrite new construction or an existing property; in either case the investors' stakes typically sell for as little as $10,000 but can go for far more. If you're a professional in your city or town, you may have been approached to invest in an apartment building or maybe a housing development this way.

The key in evaluating syndications, says Glenn Sonnenberg, president of Legg Mason Real Estate Investors in west Los Angeles, is finding one led by a general partner who has loads of experience in exactly the kind of real estate the partnership is putting its money into. Not only that, but the general partner should have experience with properties in the area where the project is located. "You need someone who has a track record and is investing alongside you," he says. Fees for the general partner generally shouldn't exceed 1 percent of the purchase price of the investment. Don't forget to demand regular quarterly reports and make sure you're comfortable locking up your money for a five- to seven-year period, the length of most deals.

"There is no secondary market in these things," says the Arizona Real Estate Center's Jay Butler. "If you feel you want to sell your partnership, it's hard to."

But a syndication will allow you to invest in bigger projects such as office buildings, apartment complexes, or retail centers that you otherwise might not be able to afford on your own. And you can invest passively without having to actually manage tenants or building maintenance yourself.

5

FINANCING YOUR INVESTMENT

O bsessing over whether you've picked exactly the wrong time to buy real estate? You're not alone. After all, existing home prices are starting to make the Nasdaq bubble look quaint. In the five years ended in mid-2002, the average existing home price has shot up 34 percent. But what is too often overlooked is the fact that it's a great time for homebuyers as well. Interest rates are at their lowest levels in 32 years. And, while they could move higher, there's little reason to believe that they will return to the double-digit levels of the early 1980s that kept so many people out of the housing market.

Lenders, meanwhile, have come up with new kinds of loans that will allow you to buy more house for your money. Can't come up with a down payment? Plenty of banks will lend you 100 percent of the value of your property. Some will lend more. Others have a program that lets you borrow against your parents' stock portfolio. The best part is that new computer programs that lenders use to evaluate your mortgage are more liberal with loan dollars than the sharp-penciled mortgage bankers who used to do the calculations by hand. In other words, while the price you end up paying for your new home may have you waking up with night sweats, low interest rates and innovative loan programs may mean you can buy more house than you imagined. Says Keith Gumbinger, vice president of mortgage data publisher HSH Associates, "The credit spigots are wide open."

You can rely on overworked loan officers to show you the ins and outs of these computerized programs, or the best ways to stretch your mortgage dollar. But that's not too likely. Consider this chapter Finance 101 for real estate. Once you've learned how the process works, we'll acquaint you with the different mortgage products on offer and show you the typical mistakes aspiring homeowners make on their mortgage applications; you'll also find out exactly how much home you can afford. If you're buying your property for investment purposes, we'll guide you through the mysterious world of commercial real estate finance and show you the key tax issues you'll need to consider before you sign on the dotted line.

How a Lender Looks at Your Application

Not that long ago, when lenders considered whether to approve a mortgage applicant for a loan, the crux of their decision came down to just two numbers: the consumer's housing expense and total obligation ratios. The first, the housing expense ratio, sets a ceiling on how much of your gross monthly income you can spend on your monthly mortgage payment, including principal, interest, property taxes, and homeowner's insurance. The other, the total obligation ratio, adds your debt to your housing expenses to set an upper limit on all of your obligations. Traditionally, on loans under $240,000, also called "conforming" loans, the caps have been 28 percent of monthly gross income for housing expenses and 36 percent for overall debt. For bigger loans, or "jumbo" loans, the limits are slightly higher, about 33 percent for housing and 38 percent for total obligation.

While those ratios continue to be good rules of thumb, they aren't the keys to predicting whether you'll get the loan amount you want. Far more important to bankers is your credit history. If you have good credit, the increasing use of computerized systems that assign you a "credit score" may make it easier to get a bigger mortgage, even if you carry a lot of debt. Contrary to what you may have thought, credit scoring systems—which, among other things, evaluate how extended you are on your credit and whether you pay bills on time—can be your friend. A high credit score means you're more likely to pay your mortgage on time, and that's what lenders really care about.

Today, bankers and mortgage brokers say these computerized programs allow lenders to be more liberal in doling out mortgage dollars than evaluations done by humans. Tim Debany, a mortgage broker at Landmark Financial Group in Southport, Connecticut, says he's seen individuals with excellent credit ratings get approved for loans even when the mortgage debt will drive the borrower's total obligation ratio to 70 percent. The key is credit history, says Tom Quinn, director of myFICO (www.myfico.com), the web site of Fair, Isaac and Company, developers of one of the most widely used credit scoring systems. "Even if you're not a millionaire," he says, "if you've demonstrated you can handle your debt, there's a good chance that you can get a loan that previously a banker may have decided your income wasn't high enough to meet." (See Worksheet 5.1.)

These days, it's not just the credit analysis that is automated. Many lenders use automated underwriting programs, too, to evaluate applications of potential homebuyers. The benefit of all this techno-logical improvement to prospective homeowners? Speed. Borrowers can get preliminary approvals nearly instantaneously, and in a hot real estate market that can be a deal maker.

Quinn, who helped create some of Fair, Isaac's credit scoring sys-tems, says there are three main elements that go into the model: the buyer's application information, the debt and total obligation ratios, and the credit score. The credit score is now used in more than 75 percent of mortgage decisions, and gives lenders a sense of the likeli-hood that a borrower will repay the loan.

Two things drive your credit score: your past bill-paying record and how extended you are on your available credit. If you have prob-lems with either of these, by all means take steps to make your credit report look better. Remember, your report focuses on current habits, not what happened in the past. "Every time your credit report—and score—is pulled," says Quinn, "the model rescores. Let's say it's been a year since you applied for a loan—a new score is generated based on

How Much House Can You Afford?

Step One

To start, figure out how much money you can borrow.

1. Gross monthly salary $_____

2. Bonuses, commissions, overtime, previous two years $_____

3. Divide line 2 by 24 $_____

4. Add lines 1 and 3 $_____

This is your total monthly "qualifying income."

5. Estimated monthly property tax payments and
   homeowner's insurance on a new home.
   (Call local tax assessor's office for property tax estimate;
   for homeowner's insurance, use the national average
   of $35 a month.) $_____

6. Multiply line 4 by 0.28 $_____

7. Subtract line 5 from line 6 $_____

*This is how much you can afford to pay per month under the
"housing ratio."*

8. Multiply line 4 by 0.36 $_____

9. Monthly debt: credit cards, car loans, student loans, child
   support/alimony $_____

10. Subtract lines 5 and 9 from line 8 $_____

*This is how much you can afford to pay per month under the
"total obligation ratio."*

11. Compare lines 7 and 10. The lesser amount is the approximate
    monthly mortgage payment for which you can qualify.
    To see how big a loan you can get with that payment,
    use the table in Worksheet 5.2 and enter the amount
    here $_____

WORKSHEET 5.1   How Much House Can You Afford?

Step Two
Naturally, the bigger the down payment you make, the more house you can afford. But don't worry. Many lenders will take less than 20 percent.

1. Estimate equity in your current home. (Today's value minus your mortgage balance. If you're a first-time homebuyer, skip to line 6.) $_____

2. Enter repairs needed before selling $_____

3. Enter closing costs. (These vary widely. Multiply selling price by 3 percent for a rough estimate.) $_____

4. Enter broker's commission on sale of your current home. (Commission ranges from 5 to 8 percent of sale price.) $_____

5. Subtract lines 2, 3, and 4 from line 1 $_____

6. Enter additional savings you're prepared to put toward a down payment $_____

7. Add lines 5 and 6 $_____

This is the total amount you have available for a down payment.

8. Maximum amount you can borrow, from line 11 in Step One $_____

9. Divide line 8 by 0.80 $_____

This is how much house you can afford right now, assuming a 20 percent down payment. For a 10 percent down payment, divide line 8 by 0.90. If you're putting only 5 percent down, divide by 0.95.

10. Subtract line 8 from line 9 $_____

This is the down payment you'll have to come up with for the house on line 9. If this amount is less than the amount on line 7, add lines 7 and 8. This is how much you can afford to spend on a house.

WORKSHEET 5.1   *(Continued)*

your latest information." For starters, if you're overextended on your credit, don't try to open new credit card accounts before you apply for a mortgage. "It makes it look like you are trying to get more credit," says Quinn. "It may lower your score." Likewise, don't cancel cards or accounts, since the models disregard accounts that have been inactive for a long period of time.

And if you're one of the conscientious few who refuse to revolve—that is, you pay off your credit card balances each and every month—you may find that doing so gives you precious little help with your mortgage application. That's because the computer program is simply looking to determine whether you make regular payments on time. Of course, even if you consistently repay your cards, your score will still suffer if you're charging the maximum allowable on your cards each month.

Remember: Credit scores are based on data fed to the reporting agencies by large companies with the computer systems in place to closely monitor creditors. That means your record on credit cards and auto loans will get far more scrutiny than your history of paying your utility bills or student loans.

Fix Your Credit Report

Now that you know how lenders evaluate your creditworthiness, you'll want to review your credit report for any errors. Get a copy from one of the three major credit bureaus at their web sites—Equifax (www.equifax.com), Experian (www.experian.com), or TransUnion (www.transunion.com). Residents of Colorado, Georgia, Maryland, Massachusetts, New Jersey, and Vermont can get these reports for free. To get all three reports at one go, suggests Mike Kidwell, co-founder of online debt-counseling service Myvesta (www.myvesta.org), point your browser to the TrueCredit site at www.truecredit.com ($34.95). Credit scores cost an additional $4.95.

Scan each of these reports carefully for an error. If there's a mistake—and Kidwell says about half the reports he sees contain errors—

write a protest letter to the credit bureau, not the collection agency, or fill out the dispute form you get with your credit report. Ask for an investigation. Send proof by certified mail that you've paid off the debt or that it's not yours. The bureau has 30 days to respond to your complaint. If the credit bureau still insists that the debt is yours, write the creditor directly asking for proof. Keep in mind that many of these mistakes are simple inputting errors; others, failures to update old information. Copy any correspondence to your mortgage broker or lender to keep them apprised. And give yourself some time. Even if you make all the right moves, clearing up an erroneous credit report can take months.

These days the bureaus also sell the one factor bankers rely on most in evaluating borrowers—credit scores. The most widely used, the FICO score, is available at both the myFICO and Equifax web sites. You'll want to make sure to interpret these numbers correctly. Scores of 700 and up are considered excellent. Lenders will give you an A rating if your score is top of the class, and you'll also have access to the best interest rates. According to Myvesta, 60 percent of the U.S. population earns these marks. Scoring 600 to 699 is still good, but ranks a B rating, which means you'll pay a little more in interest on your loan. Typically people scoring in this range have been a few days late with a payment or simply don't have much of a credit history. If you score in this range, you join about 27 percent of the U.S. population.

A score of 500 to 599 tells creditors that you may have been 60 days late on credit cards or other bills, or on your mortgage payments. There might be a collection agency hounding you for payment on an account. That means you'll pay two percentage points or more over what borrowers with excellent credit records are paying. Just 12 percent of the population falls into this category.

If you score below 499, it means you have liens against your property or you may have been sued for missed payments by a lender. You may even have a foreclosure in your history. Believe it or not, you are still eligible for a loan, but be prepared to pay at least three percentage points more than people with the best credit.

Turn In an Error-Free Application

If you're trying for your dream home, the last thing you want to do is make a mistake on your mortgage application. But it happens more often than you would think. Even simple things like income can get confusing. Most people think estimating their annual income on a mortgage application is as simple as copying their gross wages from their W-2 forms. Not so. Copying those numbers could lead you to make the single biggest error made by mortgage applicants—overestimating income.

To avoid such an error, make sure that any portion of your income that comes from bonuses or other incentive pay is realistic. The easiest way to do that is simply to average your bonuses from the past two years and add that amount to your base salary. If most of your income is commission-based, you could be in trouble when it comes to getting a loan—especially if you've been very clever about reducing your income for tax purposes by deducting loads of expenses. Lenders will generally average two years' worth of expenses and deduct that amount. If expenses cancel out virtually all of your income, though, you may be faced with paying a slightly higher mortgage rate to get a "no documentation" loan. That means you don't have to submit to the qualifying process as long as you can come up with a 10 to 20 percent down payment and your credit quality is pristine. By the way, "no documentation" is a bit of a misnomer. You'll still have to provide a credit report and a property appraisal.

Another easy mistake to make: underestimating the amount of property tax you'll have to pay each month on your castle. Even if you haven't picked out the house you plan to buy, you still should make an estimate of taxes. Since towns even in the same county can levy taxes at very different rates, you'll want to take extra care to get this number right. For example, owners of a typical single-family home in Weston, Connecticut, costing $600,000 would face $8,000 in taxes, while neighbors across the border in Westport might pay only $5,500, says Landmark's Debany. The difference? Westport has more businesses paying local taxes; hence individual property owners pay less. To get the most accurate tax estimate, pick a house in a neighborhood you like that is similar in size to the one you hope to buy. Then call or visit the local tax assessor's office for the annual tax bill for that house, or ask a local real estate broker.

Remember: Credit scoring companies may not pay much attention to your student loans, but you'll be obliged to report them and other monthly debts you face in your mortgage application. In addition to car and college loans, other revolving debts you'll want to report to your banker (they'll likely be found anyway) include alimony, child support payments, and even 401(k) debt. To figure your monthly credit card debt on the application, you can take 3 percent of your average balance.

Before adding any of these debts to your application, though, understand that loans or bills that will be paid off in 10 months or less—a car loan, for instance—shouldn't be included, nor should payments for life insurance or health insurance coverage. The rationale? If you stopped paying for that insurance, you wouldn't owe any money, even though you also wouldn't have any coverage. Other monthly obligations your lender doesn't care about are telephone, utility, and cable bills.

To estimate homeowner's insurance, use the national average of $35 a month as a ballpark figure. Don't forget to add in your mortgage insurance costs if you were unable to come up with a 20 percent down payment, and any condominium fees.

You'll also have to estimate loan origination, attorney, and title fees, also known as the closing costs. (Some states may tack on other fees as well.) For a rough estimate of what your closing costs might be, multiply your selling price by 3 percent. Or you can ask a lender, who will often give you a good-faith estimate on closing costs even if you don't apply for a loan. (See Worksheet 5.2.)

Getting Together the Down Payment

Ask anyone: Scrounging up a 20 percent down payment for a home whose value has been rising rapidly for several years is no easy task. And that's exactly the situation many homeowners find themselves in. Lenders, though, have come up with a spate of low down payment and no down payment programs that can help you out. Plenty of lenders offer loans for *over 100 percent* of the purchase price. HSH Associates' Gumbinger says the extra interest that you'll pay for a 100 percent plus loan is only a quarter to a half point over conventional mortgage rates. The real risk of using one of these loans? If the market turns sour, you could end up owing more than your house is worth. And without a 20 percent down payment you'll be paying mortgage insurance that protects your lender in case you default on the loan.

One way to avoid paying mortgage insurance is to obtain a piggyback loan to bridge the gap between the amount you're able to come up with and the 20 percent the bank requires. Here's how it works: Let's say you can only put down, as an example, 10 percent. The mortgage is then structured into two pieces: an 80 percent first mortgage and a 10 percent second mortgage, home equity loan, or home equity line of credit. You avoid paying mortgage insurance,

How Big a Loan Can You Qualify For?

Match your maximum monthly payment (principal and interest) as closely as possible with a dollar amount shown at the bottom of the columns in Table 5.1. Then choose a term—15 or 30 years—and an interest rate. (You can get current interest rates offered by banks in your area and national lenders at www.hsh.com.) Where those three variables intersect is the amount you can borrow, in thousands. *Note:* If your maximum monthly payment is off the chart—$3,500, say—you can still use the table. In this case, simply find the term and interest rate you want at $1,750 a month and multiply the amount you find by two.

WORKSHEET 5.2   How Big a Loan Can You Qualify For?

TABLE 5.1 YOUR BORROWING POWER*

Interest Rate	15 Years	30 Years	15 Years	30 Years	15 Years	30 Years	15 Years	30 Years	15 Years	30 Years
5.00%	$94.8	$139.7	$126.5	$186.2	$158.0	$232.8	$189.6	$279.4	$221.2	$325.9
5.13	94.0	137.7	125.4	183.6	156.7	229.5	188.1	275.4	219.4	321.4
5.25	93.2	135.8	124.3	181.0	155.4	226.3	186.5	271.6	217.6	316.9
5.38	92.5	133.9	123.3	178.5	154.2	223.2	185.0	267.8	215.9	312.5
5.50	91.7	132.0	122.3	176.1	152.9	220.1	183.5	264.1	214.1	308.2
5.63	91.0	130.2	121.3	173.7	151.7	217.1	182.0	260.5	212.5	304.0
5.75	90.3	128.5	120.4	171.3	150.5	214.1	180.6	257.0	210.7	299.8
5.88	89.5	126.7	119.4	169.0	149.3	211.3	179.1	253.5	209.0	295.8
6.00	88.8	125.0	118.5	166.7	148.1	208.4	177.7	250.1	207.3	291.8
6.13	88.1	123.4	117.5	164.5	146.9	205.7	176.3	246.8	205.7	288.0
6.25	87.4	121.8	116.6	162.4	145.7	203.0	174.9	243.6	204.1	284.2
6.38	86.7	120.2	115.7	160.2	144.6	200.3	173.5	240.4	202.4	280.6
6.50	86.0	118.6	114.7	158.2	143.4	200.3	172.1	237.3	200.8	276.8
6.63	85.4	117.1	113.8	156.1	142.3	195.2	170.8	234.2	199.3	273.3
6.75	84.7	115.6	113.0	154.1	141.2	192.7	169.5	231.2	197.7	269.8
6.88	84.0	114.1	112.1	152.2	140.1	190.2	168.1	228.3	196.2	266.3
7.00	83.4	112.7	111.2	150.3	139.0	187.8	166.8	225.4	194.6	263.0
7.13	82.7	111.3	110.3	148.4	137.9	185.5	165.5	222.6	193.1	259.7
7.25	82.1	109.9	109.5	146.5	136.9	183.2	164.3	219.8	191.7	256.5
7.38	81.5	108.5	108.7	144.7	135.8	180.9	163.0	217.1	190.2	253.3
	$750/Month		$1,000/Month		$1,250/Month		$1,500/Month		$1,750/Month	

* Except for interest rates, numbers are in thousands.

(Continued)

79

TABLE 5.1 (Continued)

Interest Rate	15 Years	30 Years	15 Years	30 Years	15 Years	30 Years	15 Years	30 Years	15 Years	30 Years
7.50%	$80.9	$107.2	$107.8	$143.0	$134.8	$178.7	$161.8	$214.5	$188.7	$250.2
7.63	80.2	105.9	107.0	141.2	133.8	176.6	160.5	211.9	187.3	247.2
7.75	79.6	104.6	106.2	139.5	132.7	174.4	159.3	209.3	185.9	244.2
7.88	79.0	103.4	105.4	137.9	131.7	172.3	158.1	206.8	184.5	241.3
8.00	78.4	102.2	104.6	136.2	130.8	170.3	156.9	204.4	183.1	238.4
8.13	77.8	101.0	103.8	134.6	129.8	168.3	155.7	202.0	181.7	235.6
8.25	77.3	99.8	103.0	133.1	128.8	166.3	154.6	199.6	180.3	232.9
8.38	76.7	98.6	102.3	131.5	127.8	164.4	153.5	197.3	179.0	230.2
8.50	76.1	97.5	101.5	130.0	126.9	162.5	152.3	195.0	177.7	227.5
8.63	75.5	96.4	100.7	128.5	125.9	160.7	151.1	192.8	176.3	224.9
8.75	75.0	95.3	100.0	127.1	125.0	158.8	150.0	190.6	175.0	222.4
8.88	74.4	94.2	99.3	125.6	124.1	157.1	148.9	188.5	173.8	219.9
9.00	73.9	93.2	98.5	124.2	123.2	155.3	147.8	186.4	172.5	217.4
9.13	73.4	92.1	97.8	122.9	122.3	153.6	146.8	184.3	171.2	215.0
9.25	72.8	91.1	97.1	121.5	121.4	151.9	145.7	182.3	170.0	212.7
9.38	72.3	90.1	96.4	120.2	120.5	150.2	144.6	180.3	168.8	210.3
9.50	71.8	89.1	95.7	118.9	119.7	148.6	143.6	178.3	167.5	208.1
9.63	71.3	88.2	95.0	117.6	118.8	147.0	142.6	176.4	166.3	205.8
9.75	70.7	87.2	94.3	116.3	117.9	145.4	141.4	174.5	165.1	203.6
9.88	70.2	86.3	93.7	115.1	117.5	143.9	140.5	172.7	164.0	201.5
	$750/Month		$1,000/Month		$1,250/Month		$1,500/Month		$1,750/Month	

Interest Rate	15 Years	30 Years	15 Years	30 Years	15 Years	30 Years	15 Years	30 Years	15 Years	30 Years
5.00%	$252.9	$372.5	$284.5	$418.1	$316.1	$465.7	$347.7	$512.2	$379.3	$558.8
5.13	250.8	367.3	282.1	413.2	313.5	459.1	344.9	505	376.2	550.9
5.25	248.7	362.1	279.8	407.4	310.9	452.7	342.0	498.0	373.1	543.2
5.38	246.7	357.1	277.6	401.8	308.4	446.4	339.3	491.0	370.1	535.7
5.50	244.7	352.2	275.3	396.2	305.9	440.3	336.5	484.3	367.1	528.3
5.63	242.7	347.4	273.1	390.8	303.4	434.2	333.8	477.7	364.1	521.1
5.75	240.8	342.7	271.8	385.5	301.0	428.3	331.1	471.2	361.2	514.0
5.88	238.9	338.1	268.7	380.3	298.6	422.6	328.5	464.8	358.3	507.1
6.00	237.0	333.5	266.6	375.2	296.2	416.9	325.8	458.6	355.5	500.3
6.13	235.1	329.1	264.5	370.3	293.9	411.4	323.2	452.5	352.6	493.7
6.25	233.2	324.8	262.4	365.4	291.5	406.0	320.7	446.6	349.8	487.2
6.38	231.4	320.5	260.3	360.6	289.2	400.7	318.1	440.7	347.1	480.8
6.50	229.5	316.4	258.2	355.9	286.9	395.5	315.6	435.0	344.3	474.6
6.63	227.7	312.3	256.2	351.3	284.7	390.4	313.2	429.4	341.6	468.5
6.75	226.0	309.9	254.2	346.9	282.5	385.4	310.7	423.9	339.0	462.5
6.88	224.2	304.4	252.2	342.5	280.3	380.5	308.3	418.6	336.3	456.6
7.00	222.5	300.6	250.3	338.1	278.1	375.7	305.9	413.3	333.7	450.9
7.13	220.7	296.8	248.3	333.9	275.9	371.0	303.5	408.1	331.1	445.2
7.25	219.0	293.1	256.4	329.9	273.8	366.4	301.2	403.1	328.6	439.7
7.38	217.4	289.5	244.5	325.7	271.7	361.9	298.9	398.1	326.3	434.3
	$2,000/Month		$2,250/Month		$2,500/Month		$2,750/Month		$3,000/Month	

(Continued)

TABLE 5.1 (Continued)

Interest Rate	$2,000/Month		$2,250/Month		$2,500/Month		$2,750/Month		$3,000/Month	
	15 Years	30 Years	15 Years	30 Years	15 Years	30 Years	15 Years	30 Years	15 Years	30 Years
7.50%	$215.7	$286.0	$242.7	$321.7	$269.6	$357.5	$296.6	$393.2	$323.6	$429.0
7.63	214.1	282.5	240.8	317.8	267.6	353.2	294.3	388.5	321.1	423.8
7.75	212.4	279.1	239.0	314.0	265.5	348.9	292.1	383.8	318.7	418.7
7.88	210.8	275.8	237.2	310.3	263.5	344.7	289.9	379.2	316.3	413.7
8.00	209.2	272.5	235.4	306.6	261.6	340.7	287.7	374.7	313.9	408.8
8.13	207.7	269.3	233.6	303.0	259.6	336.7	285.6	370.3	311.5	404.0
8.25	206.1	266.2	231.9	299.4	257.6	332.7	283.4	366.0	309.2	399.3
8.38	204.6	263.1	230.1	296.0	255.7	328.9	281.3	361.8	306.9	394.6
8.50	203.0	260.1	228.4	292.6	253.8	325.1	279.2	357.6	304.6	390.1
8.63	201.5	257.1	226.7	289.2	251.9	321.4	277.1	353.5	302.3	385.7
8.75	200.1	254.2	225.1	286.0	250.1	317.7	275.1	349.5	300.1	381.3
8.88	198.6	251.3	223.4	282.7	248.3	314.2	273.1	345.6	297.9	377.0
9.00	197.1	248.5	221.8	279.6	246.4	310.7	271.1	341.7	295.7	372.8
9.13	195.7	245.8	220.2	276.5	244.6	307.2	269.1	337.9	293.6	368.7
9.25	194.3	243.1	218.6	273.4	242.9	303.8	267.1	334.2	291.4	364.6
9.38	192.9	240.4	217.0	270.5	241.1	300.5	265.2	330.6	289.3	360.6
9.50	191.5	237.8	215.4	267.5	239.1	297.3	263.3	327.0	287.2	356.7
9.63	190.1	235.2	213.9	264.7	237.6	294.1	261.4	323.5	285.2	352.9
9.75	188.7	232.7	212.3	261.8	235.9	290.9	259.5	320.0	283.1	349.1
9.88	187.4	230.3	210.8	259.1	234.3	287.9	257.7	316.6	281.1	345.4
P & I	$2,000/Month		$2,250/Month		$2,500/Month		$2,750/Month		$3,000/Month	

Source: HSH Associates, www.HSH.com.

which is based on the first mortgage. True, you'll most likely pay a slightly higher interest rate on the second mortgage (one to two percentage points above conventional mortgage rates), but you can always pay it off earlier. A piggyback mortgage can also help you avoid the higher interest rates associated with a jumbo mortgage, if you can keep that first mortgage under $240,000. The downside of a piggyback loan, says Gumbinger, is that it can limit your borrowing capabilities.

Piggybacks aren't the only option for people struggling with a down payment. There's always Mummy and Daddy. Merrill Lynch offers a loan it calls Parent Power, which allows children to use their parents' stock portfolio to help them with a down payment. Essentially, the stock is pledged as a guarantee for a portion of the loan amount. The stocks aren't sold, but held in the parents' portfolio so that capital gains taxes are delayed.

If your problem is that your earnings are paid in cash, Wells Fargo has a program that can help. The West Coast bank has expanded its qualifying guidelines to include secondary income received in cash, such as pay from cleaning service, child care, or seasonal work. So, instead of having to provide verifiable W-2 income to qualify for a loan, borrowers could use a broader range of income sources.

Those aren't the only options out there. You'll naturally have to make a choice between a fixed rate mortgage and an adjustable rate mortgage (ARM). The rate difference between the two as of September 2002 was 1.75 percentage points, making an ARM extremely attractive to buyers trying to stretch their mortgage dollars. But the downside to an adjustable rate is that the rate resets every year after an introductory period that typically lasts one, three, or five years. And, with rates hovering at lows, the likely direction of rates is higher, rather than lower. However, adjustable rate loans make sense for some people. If you absolutely, positively plan to be in your home for a short period of time, say five years or less, then an adjustable rate may make sense. A typical ARM buyer might be an executive who moves every three years or a soon-to-be retiree who expects to downsize. Just make sure you know exactly how often the rate adjusts and which benchmark your rate will be tied to.

Where to Get Your Mortgage

Just a short while ago, the Web was going to revolutionize the mortgage business. There'd be one-click refinancing, instant loan approvals, and market-beating rates. But that just hasn't happened—not even close. Many mortgage web sites haven't survived the dot-com meltdown. Lenders still require paper for proof of assets and employment. As for price, "There's no difference in the cost of funds online and offline," says Richard Beidl, an independent consultant to financial services companies.

Here's what the Internet is really good for: Find the best interest rate online, then use that information to put the stranglehold on your own (earthbound) lender or mortgage broker. Bankrate.com offers the most comprehensive free rate comparisons and posts daily averages for 15- and 30-year fixed and adjustable loans from nearly 4,000 institutions.

Where can this comparison shopping get you? The average rate for a 30-year fixed mortgage in Philadelphia in the summer of 2002 was 6.47 percent (with 0.12 in points payable at closing). So on a loan of $200,000, the monthly payment would be $1,260. The best rate Bankrate.com showed was 5.75 percent, with a monthly payment of $1,167. That's a saving of $93 per month, or about $33,480 over the term of the loan. If you don't yet have a lender to strangle, Bankrate.com lists them, organized by state, as does Gumbinger's HSH Associates (www.hsh.com).

Where Are Rates Headed?

It's all too easy to get obsessed with interest rates as you prepare to lock in one for your new mortgage. You scan the headlines, watch for any comment from the Federal Reserve chairman, and even start reading the agate print in your newspaper. But contrary to what you may have thought, the Federal Reserve has little to do with determining the interest rate you'll pay on your home mortgage. It's mortgage bankers who decide where to set rates, and for the most part they track the 10-year Treasury note. In other words, if rates on these long-term government securities rise, so will mortgage rates; if they plunge, mortgage rates will do the same.

Lately homebuyers have had plenty of opportunities to lock in a luscious 30-year rate (it slid to a 32-year low in the fall of 2002). Few generations have had things so good. The highest level for mortgage rates in recent memory was 15.98 percent back in 1981 (and the average borrower had to pay a fee of up to two percentage points of the loan's value to boot). The near-term average, however, has been closer to 8 percent. (See Figure 5.1.) Trying to predict where these rates are going, though, is no easy matter. One place to look for educated guesses? Bankrate.com, which each week publishes the 30-day forecasts of several prominent mortgage bankers.

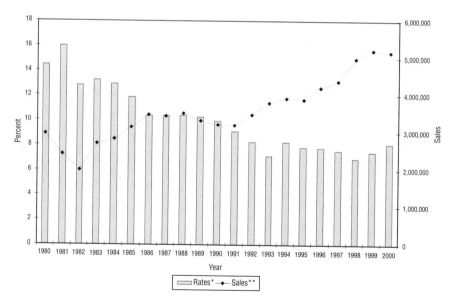

FIGURE 5.1   The Path of Mortgage Rates
*30-year fixed mortgage rates. *Source:* Bankrate.com. Reprinted with permission.
**U.S. sales, existing homes. *Source:* National Association of Realtors. Reprinted with permission.

Getting the Loan for an Investment

If you're at all familiar with the basics of home mortgages, you know this: Getting a home loan in recent years has been a piece of cake for most families, unless, of course, they had a checkered credit history. Don't expect such easy pickings if you plan to buy a property for investment purposes. That's because bankers evaluate investment property loans completely differently from mortgage loans for a primary home. "The guidelines are more conservative because you don't have an owner-occupied property with an on-site owner maintaining the property," says Chet DeStefano, mortgage market leader for the Northeast region at Wachovia Bank. "You have tenants, and there is an inherent risk of loss of rental income and damage to property. Delinquency rates are higher for investment property than owner occupied."

For those reasons, first-time buyers of investment property find the terms offered by conventional bankers far less attractive than they might have imagined. If you go directly to a bank loan officer, many will lend only 75 percent to 80 percent of the property's value, although occasional 90 percent loans can be found. In addition, you'll pay a higher interest rate. Wells Fargo, for example, charges a half point to a full point higher interest rate on investment property loans than on mortgages for primary residences. Be prepared to have three to four months of expenses on hand, everything from utilities to mortgage costs. Moreover, depending on the loan program and other variables, buyers may be asked to pay one to one and a half points (one point is equal to 1 percent of the mortgage) more for an investment property.

One hurdle you can't avoid regardless of the lender: the appraisal. If you're already a homeowner, you probably regard this step as a snap. After all, homeowners know that appraisals are pretty much perfunctory; it's rare that an appraiser challenges the agreed-upon purchase price for a home. But in a real estate purchase for investment, bankers are more demanding because the property has to produce the cash flow to make mortgage payments each month. For that reason, you can expect the appraiser to evaluate rental income and expenses to determine the likelihood of whether you'll have to dip into your own pocket to pay the mortgage.

But you don't have to settle for such terms. The best strategy is to shop around for a mortgage lender. Start by contacting smaller banks and savings and loans familiar with your local market. Local institutions are the best choice if you're buying a second home you intend to rent out or even a multifamily house with four or fewer apartments. A second option is a mortgage broker, who can quickly tap a number of banks that might finance your property. Using a broker makes sense if you're new to the market or if you've had difficulty in the past putting together financing. Keep in mind, though, that brokers are simply intermediaries hooking you up with people who will ultimately finance your deal.

Another option? Mortgage bankers. These people are lenders who usually originate home loans from their own funds and then resell the loans. Bankers can help fund larger properties like strip centers or larger apartment complexes, but many also handle smaller multifamily buildings. To find a mortgage banker in your area, go to the web site of the Mortgage Bankers Association of America at www.mbaa.org. You'll notice that some of the bankers are units of larger companies, like General Motors. Our advice: Smaller companies are more likely to handle deals under $1 million, and they typically know the local terrain better. Jim Murphy, chairman of New England Realty Resources, located in Boston, is relentlessly local. "I never do a deal outside of New England," he says. "If you tell me where a property is, chances are I'll have some knowledge of the market." Of course, the expertise doesn't come for free. Murphy charges a fee of 1 percent of the loan amount for his services.

It's all a lot less daunting than it sounds. Consider the case of Joe Tiago of Bridgeport, Connecticut. Tiago was just 24 and living at his parents' house when he decided to buy his first investment property, a $75,000 three-unit building. He first contacted his own bank for a loan, but was told he would need a cosigner because of his relative inexperience. Tiago balked. Although he says he "didn't have a big bank account," he could produce a pristine credit record and solid employment history driving a concrete truck. So he next sought out a mortgage broker in a nearby town to find out if there was any way to get a loan on his own. Not only did he succeed, but he also managed to get a loan for 90 percent of the value of the property. Once he established a record paying his mortgage on time, he had no trouble getting his second, third, and fourth loans, scouting new properties each time rents from his current buildings paid back his down payment. Now he spends all of his time managing his properties, and is preparing to start building homes with his brother.

When it comes to financing your investment, it pays to be creative. If you're buying a single-family home that you intend to rent out, Robert Bruss, an investor who writes a real estate newsletter (it can be ordered at www.bobbruss.com), suggests that you may be able to get so-called carryback financing. This sort of loan is provided by the *owner* of the property, thereby allowing you, the borrower, to skip the usual credit checks—and set your own loan terms. Remember, half of all homes are actually owned free and clear. When the sellers do put these properties on the market, it's often because they are ready to retire and are eager to cash out of their homes to bankroll their golden years. Bruss says they may well regard an offer to pay 7 percent on their money as a solid investment when certificates of deposit are paying in the low single digits. What's more, if they still owe money on their house they may be willing to have you take over their mortgage. Bruss says homes that are vacant and have been on the market for 30 days or more are good candidates for such deals.

How Much Investment Property Can You Afford?

It's hard enough figuring out what kind of property you should buy; should it be apartments or office space, a single-family home or a strip center? But even that decision pales in comparison to the amount you decide to pay for your moneymaker. Experienced investors say the single biggest mistake that first-time investors make is paying too much for a property whose rental income stream can't support such a price. "New investors are surprised to find how competitive commercial real estate can be," says New England Realty's Murphy. "You'll be shocked at what people will pay. For the small investor, people are willing to take returns that would surprise you."

To prevent yourself from getting pressured into a deal that's simply too rich, you need to understand how the professionals evaluate prices. The most common approach is called income capitalization. That sounds complex, but in fact it's pretty simple. First off, you'll need to estimate net operating income for the property by subtracting annual costs—including insurance, property taxes, maintenance, reserves, and utilities—from the gross annual rents (plus any additional income you can pick up at the property). The price you pay should be equal to the net operating income divided by the rate of return on capital experienced by most real estate investors in your area. That rate of return on capital, which is called the capitalization (cap) rate, is a figure that most loan professionals will be familiar with. Since cap rates can vary, ask your commercial real estate agent and lender what rates apply in your area. Most lenders advise first-time investors to demand a cap rate of 10 percent at minimum. You can also run your own calculation using prices and net operating income estimates from your agent.

Of course, the key to arriving at the right price is plugging in the most accurate numbers possible. Many landlords, particularly those truly interested in selling their properties, either will let you see their rental agreements and utility bills so that you can get truly accurate expense figures, or may even show you a Schedule E from their tax returns that will detail expenses from their properties. If the seller isn't cooperative or if you want to know whether rents could be raised at the property you're thinking about buying, your best source of rent information may well be the classified ads in your Sunday newspaper (see Table 5.2). Check out rents offered at comparable buildings in the neighborhood. Local apartment associations can be a useful guide, says one San Francisco investor, but their numbers can be behind the curve. "In the first building we bought, we knew we could get $1,000 more per unit month than the previous owners were charging just by

TABLE 5.2   THE PATH OF RENT GROWTH

Market	2Q 2002 Asking Rent	Asking Rent Growth Since 1990
Cleveland	$653	30.3%
Milwaukee	763	32.5
Detroit	776	35.0
Pittsburgh	720	37.4
Indianapolis	611	38.9
Portland	711	39.1
Norfolk	631	39.6
Columbus	613	39.6
St. Louis	635	40.2
Baltimore	763	41.6
Los Angeles	1,074	41.7
Chicago	943	44.0
Orlando	730	44.0
Philadelphia	840	45.3
Kansas City	635	47.3
Palm Beach	934	48.0
Fort Lauderdale	924	50.0
Memphis	595	52.2
Minneapolis	870	52.6
Sacramento	812	52.6
Median	**770**	**52.6**
Charlotte	716	52.7
Orange County, California	1,196	52.7
Tampa–St. Petersburg	704	53.4
Jacksonville	685	53.9
District of Columbia	1,060	55.4

(Continued)

TABLE 5.2   *(Continued)*

Market	2Q 2002 Asking Rent	Asking Rent Growth Since 1990
Average	$ 878	55.4%
Houston	655	57.5
Miami	913	57.7
Atlanta	813	57.9
San Antonio	600	60.0
Seattle	884	60.1
San Diego	1,037	60.5
Phoenix	675	63.0
Dallas	741	69.6
San Jose	1,422	79.1
Boston	1,518	79.6
New York	2,112	93.1
San Francisco	1,615	93.6
Fairfield County, Connecticut	1,582	101.3
Denver	824	103.0
Austin	778	106.4

Source: REIS, a national commercial real estate information provider. © Reis, Inc., 2002. Reprinted with permission of Reis, Inc. All rights reserved.

looking at the ads and anecdotal stories from neighbors," he says. "Statistics are published on what happened in the past; it doesn't necessarily reflect what's happening on the street." When calculating net income, make sure to include costs for trash pickup, maintenance, and repairs. Keep in mind that many lenders will require that you have three to four months' worth of expenses on hand, just in case.

Cap rates aren't the only technique for pegging a building's ideal value. Another way to calculate it is by determining a "gross rent multiplier" implied by area rents. Let's say you're thinking about buying a home in your neighborhood to rent out. First off, you'll want to find an average rent charged by landlords of homes in that area that are similar in size and amenities. That gives you an idea of what kind of rent you'll be likely to charge. Next, gather recent sales prices of homes in the area. (Domania's web site can supply purchase prices in most parts of the United States.) Then, divide the sales price by the monthly rent. The result is the gross rent multiplier. Take an average of the gross rent multipliers in each deal so that you can get a good base for comparison. You can now use that number to figure out the appropriate price for the home in your crosshairs. Simply multiply the gross rent multiplier by the average monthly rent you calculated.

No doubt you'll also want to be able to compare your returns to the results of other assets you hold, like stocks or bonds. To do that, start by calculating your before-tax cash flow by subtracting your total annual mortgage payments and other costs from net operating income. Now, divide the cash flow by your planned down payment. The result is the return on your cash investment.

Uncle Sam's Share

Back in the mid-1980s, investors used to snap up real estate with the idea of racking up as much in losses as possible to reduce their own tax liabilities. Most of those benefits were swept away, however, in the tax reform of the late 1980s. The truth today is that while there are important deductions and write-offs that any real estate investor should know and take advantage of, it probably isn't incentive enough to change careers. In other words, don't buy a property with significant negative cash flows in the hope that tax breaks will turn your loser property into a winner. Here's a quick guide to tax issues that most affect real estate investors. Keep in mind, though, that every person's tax situation is different, and you'll definitely want to consult an accountant or Enrolled Agent (a person who can prepare tax forms and represent taxpayers in front of the IRS) to make sure you're complying with the very complex rules in this area. Taxes for vacation property owners will be discussed in Chapter 8.

The first thing to understand is that even if you simply buy a house to rent it out, the Internal Revenue Service (IRS) regards what you're doing as an investment activity. For that reason, you'll be able to deduct expenses from your rental income and depreciate your property similarly to the way a business would. When you sell your investment property, the IRS will generally view the gain on your building or house as a capital gain (an issue we'll get to in Chapter 8). Legitimate deductions include, but aren't limited to: mortgage interest, property taxes, depreciation, repairs, losses, utilities, cleaning supplies—even the cost of hiring a rental agent to help you get tenants, says Mark Luscombe, principal federal tax analyst at CCH, a leading provider of tax information. Keep in mind that if you live in the same building you can't deduct the portion of repair costs that applies to your apartment.

Now, it's likely after taking all these deductions that you've reduced your rental income for tax purposes to zero or possibly a loss. If you make less than $100,000, you can deduct up to $25,000 in losses against other income, say your salary or bonuses. If your adjusted gross income is more than $150,000, the deduction entirely phases out. However, the IRS allows you to save up passive losses to be applied to other tax years.

Wondering what we mean by depreciation? Well, because the IRS regards your activity as an investment, it allows you to recognize the fact that the houses or apartments you're buying are assets with limited useful lives. Like a company that has to buy equipment, your investment is presumed to wear out over a period of time. In the case of residential property, the government puts that useful life at 27.5 years. Commercial buildings like offices or warehouses have a useful life of 39 years. That means in each and every year you invest in, say, a house, you can deduct $1/_{27.5}$ of the price you paid, or 3.64 percent, from rental income. It may not sound like much, but it will matter to you when you sell your property. Here's why: In calculating your capital gains, the government requires you to adjust your original purchase price by the amount of depreciation you've written off. As that purchase price declines, your capital gains will rise. And so will your tax bill. (See Sidebar 5.1.)

Fighting the Taxman

You've just bought your new home, and *bam!* All of a sudden, you're hit with a new property assessment and a higher tax bill—the *last* thing you needed. But you don't have to sit and take it. Here's how to fight back.

First off, you need to understand how local property taxes work. Your town sets a millage rate, a number that represents how much you will owe per thousand dollars of property value. Next, officials place a value on your house, called the assessment. When towns want to raise property taxes they can either change the millage rate or reassess property values. In many towns, the reassessment happens once a decade; in others, it happens whenever there is a sale. There's not much you can do to change the millage rate, but you can fight city hall over your assessment. In fact, about half of people who take their complaint all the way to an appeals court win some sort of relief.

To complain effectively about your assessment, Randy Deal, who has worked as an assessor for more than two decades in upstate New York and maintains a web site, Assessor.com, suggests asking first for a copy of the property assessment card, sometimes called a data record. Check it carefully to make sure the information is correct. "That's the place a lot of corrections need to be made," he says, and advises if there is an error to call it to the attention of the assessor directly.

Assessors, Deal says, can be under tremendous pressure to work quickly when reviewing properties, and that can lead to mistakes. When he recently reassessed the town of Watkins Glen in Schuyler County, New York, he made all his observations from the public right of way. That left little opportunity for close inspections.

If that doesn't get you anywhere, Becky Fagg, a Lexington, South Carolina, grandmother who is leading a no-tax movement in her home state, suggests a more proactive approach. Put everything in writing, starting with a letter to the assessor in which you ask for a hearing on the assessment. She suggests coming to the hearing armed with comparable data on assessments of similar houses that will presumably show that your home shouldn't be valued as highly as the neighbors who, for example, just installed a pool or upgraded their electrical system.

"Do your research," says Fagg. "There are sweetheart deals all over the place."

Another approach? Accentuate the negative. Make a list of factors that may lower the value of your home, such as termites or structural problems. Negative factors may also be overlooked if your assessment is out-of-date: In New Jersey, for example, state guidelines suggest that towns reevaluate properties only every 10 years. Therefore, recent changes to your home might not have been taken into account. John Francis of Newton, Massachusetts, got his home's value lowered by pointing out that his house is on a busy street. "I got a 30 percent reduction [on my taxes]," he says.

SIDEBAR 5.1

6

THE RIGHT WAY TO RENOVATE

Once you've bought your home, you'll be tempted to sit back, relax, and forget about real estate for a good long while. But that would be a mistake. If you're like most homebuyers, you're nesting in a house that is on average 30 years old, exactly the age when some of the most expensive parts of the house, like the roof, windows, and siding, start to wear out. Of course, just repairing your house isn't the only reason you might consider a major renovation. In hot markets, some homeowners opt to finish the basement or build an expanded family room when buying a bigger home is out of the question because of escalating prices. Others are upgrading their homes to make them more accessible to elderly parents or to accommodate a growing family. And still others—the really forward-looking ones—are remodeling to make sure their home continues to appeal to potential buyers, even if they don't plan to sell it tomorrow.

Unless you're trained in the art of home building, undertaking any of these projects will mean hiring a general contractor, someone who can coordinate the efforts of carpenters, plumbers, electricians, and others who can make your remodeling dream come true. Here's where it gets tricky. If you thought the housing market was on fire in your town, just wait until you try to hire a contractor to handle even the simplest of jobs.

With the number of home-improvement projects in the United States up 25 percent in the past five years, according to Kermit Baker, director of the Remodeling Futures Program at Harvard University's Joint Center for Housing Studies, contractors are in high demand. And, although the home improvement industry is a $180 billion giant, it's still far from being a slickly professional enterprise. The remodeling business is populated by tiny mom-and-pop companies that can be difficult to evaluate. That means you'll need to do more than just pick up the Yellow Pages when you go to hire a general contractor.

In this chapter, we'll show you how to avoid the inevitable shoddy operators and find reputable contractors, how to manage them throughout the process, and what kinds of things you'll want to consider before even signing a contract to alter your abode.

Before we get started, though, there is just one more important point you'll want to consider: The money you spend for changes—even relatively big ones—won't filter through to your home's value dollar for dollar. For example, homeowners spend on average $5,865 to add a deck onto their house, but only 77 percent of that cost is typically recouped when the home is sold. In other words, the resale value of the deck drops to $4,498, according to *Remodeling* magazine's annual Cost vs. Value Report. (See Table 6.1 for a list of other home improvement projects and their resale values.)

So are remodeling dollars wasted? No way. Not only do you get use of the deck while you live in the home, but because more than 30 million American homes already have decks, they're very nearly considered must-haves, rather than nice extras. Making regular improvements to your castle not only makes it a more pleasant place to live, but doing so also means that down the road buyers will be less likely to see your home as stylistically or functionally obsolete. And that protects your investment. The last thing you want is to find out your home is considered hopelessly old-fashioned by potential buyers when it's too late to do much about it. "At what point are avocado appliances going to be a liability? You don't know until you put the home on the market," says Harvard's Baker.

TABLE 6.1   REMODELING: WHAT'S IT WORTH?

Job	Job Cost	Resale Value	Cost Recouped*
Major kitchen remodel, high end	$70,368	$56,137	80%
Bathroom addition	15,058	14,180	94
Bathroom remodel	9,720	8,506	88
Roof replacement	11,399	7,644	67
Window replacement	9,424	6,951	74
Basement refinish	43,112	33,911	79

*Percentage cost recouped when home is sold within one year of project completion.
Source: Remodeling magazine, "Cost vs. Value Report."

Picking a Contractor

When you set out to hire a general contractor to build an addition onto your house, you probably assume you're getting someone who has spent years learning the craft and gaining the proper credentials to saw a hole in the side of your den. In reality you could be getting a madman with a toolbox who answers to no one. That's because only 36 states have any licensing requirements for general contractors, according to the consumer division of AARP (formerly the American Association of Retired Persons). Where requirements do exist, they vary widely. In California, one of the stricter states, budding contractors must only prove their financial solvency and pass a written exam. One sample test question was this: "Where would the drain and sewer for a residential building be located?" Those loose licensing requirements help explain why the category of home-improvement services, which tend to be completed or overseen by contractors, ranks consistently in the top three on the list of consumer complaints issued by the National Association of Consumer Agency Administrators.

How should you shop for a contractor? Ask for references, of course, but don't just interview your candidate: Actually visit a job in progress to watch how the contractor works. (If your would-be contractor doesn't have a job at the time, that alone is a bad sign.) Tom Pendleton, owner of McLean, Virginia–based home inspection firm The House Inspector, offers this advice: "I have a three-year rule," he says. "Close to 95 percent of home-improvement contractors go out of business or change their name [due to consumer complaints or mismanagement] within three years, so you want a contractor who's been in business under the same name for more than three years." A good outside source for data on individual contractors: Handyman Online (www.handymanonline.com), a referral service that can connect you with contractors in your area who are legitimately licensed, carry liability insurance, and have at least three references.

Another source of reliable leads: Your town or city's building code enforcement officer. Evelyn Yancoskie, director of consumer affairs for Delaware County, Pennsylvania, says that many keep lists of reliable contractors. "They are a wealth of information," says Yancoskie. "Code enforcement officers would rather have the good contractors doing the work in their towns rather than the bad ones."

Keep in mind, too, that there is a big difference between hiring a general contractor who manages the various tradespeople needed to complete a major project, including carpenters, plumbers, and electricians, and the tradespeople who also freelance as contractors on small jobs. "The contractors who do small jobs are very good at trades but poor at running a business, and you have to be ready for that," says Tom McGinley, executive director of Peninsula Builders Exchange in San Carlos, California. "When you get to larger jobs, general contractors are businessmen. Tradesmen often don't understand the relationship they are in."

Even if you pick a great general contractor (and there are plenty of them out there), you can find yourself stuck with a novice subcontractor that can make your remodeling project a nightmare. Mark Herr, formerly an attorney with the New Jersey Division of Consumer Affairs, told *SmartMoney* magazine this tale of a family that wanted their kitchen redone in time for Easter: One night before the holiday, a subcontractor was sweating to install the garbage disposal. When asked why the job was giving him so much trouble, the worker replied, "When they showed me this morning at Home Depot, I thought I understood." The story points out a big problem: It's not just your contractor you have to worry about, but the subcontractors whom he hires to do the actual work. "You need to know in advance who the subcontractors are," Herr said. "You can't let the contractor sub anything out without your permission."

How can you avoid problem subcontractors? Visit homes in which your contractor's carpenter has done the finishing work, and if you like what you see, get it in writing that that particular subcontractor will be hired. Carpenters leave telltale signs in their wakes. Check to see if there are tight joints in the moldings, if cabinets are screwed into the walls rather than nailed, and if margins between doors and frames are even all around.

If you've solicited bids from general contractors and they would charge more than you want to spend, you may be tempted to go with what consumer protection agencies call "travelers." These are workers who approach people's homes and offer to do jobs at bargain-basement prices using leftover materials from nearby projects. Resist the offer. Travelers are a type of scam artist. In reality, if they do the job at all, they are doing shoddy work with low-grade materials and poor workmanship, says Wendy Weinberg, formerly the executive director of the National Association of Consumer Agency Administrators, leaving you worse off than before. While it sounds like common sense to be suspicious of solicitors, clearly such con artists can be convincing: Lisa Curtis, director of consumer services for the Denver district attorney's office, estimates that travelers bilk Colorado homeowners out of $20 million per year.

Everything You Need to Know about the Contract

When it's time to sign on the dotted line, most contractors will present you with a boilerplate agreement based on one created by the

American Institute of Architects. It lays out the job's details, including its scope, materials used, and, of course, a payment schedule. Not surprisingly, some contractors will set up a payment schedule that lets your money get ahead of the work. A contractor who has received 50 percent of the money for 25 percent of the work might just stop showing up as often. A better idea? Plan on paying 10 percent down, 25 percent when plumbing and electrical work are done, 25 percent after cabinets and windows, and 25 percent for flooring and painting. And don't hand over the last 15 percent on the final day. Its called "retainage," and you should keep it for 30 extra days just to make sure everything is working the way it should. In addition, if the job is big enough—say, $50,000 or more—invest in four hours of attorney fees to devise a contract that includes a fair payment plan (with retainage) and stipulates that disputes will be settled through arbitration (the quick and easy way to do it).

Mark Zarrilli, a mortgage salesman at the Bank of America, knows about the importance of slowly distributing pay. When he decided to enhance his Wall, New Jersey, home by putting in stamped concrete cobblestones around his pool, he agreed to pay nearly all the costs up front, giving $7,000 of the $11,000 cost of the job to the contractor for materials before work even started. "They brought somebody in to do the preliminary brickwork, and then played a duck-and-run game for three months," says Zarrilli. "They'd tell me the truck broke down, the wife was sick, the cement company couldn't deliver." Eventually, Zarrilli threw that contractor off the job, and then he spent several months tracking down the contractor's other customers to see whether they had had problems, too. (They did.) He then took his contractor to criminal court, and was ultimately rewarded for his hard work when the contractor admitted to theft and agreed to pay back a portion of Zarrilli's money.

While selecting a reputable general contractor is critical to getting your addition done right, remember that once workers are on the job your relationship will go far beyond employer-employee. In fact, it's more like a trial marriage. As with any nuptials there's usually a honeymoon period when customers are pleased to see the contractor and subcontractors. But eventually the strain of having strangers in your home will begin to wear on you. Without some kind of ground rules, carpenters and plasterers will tramp mud through your house, raid your refrigerator, and run up your electric bill. The best solution? Before the contractor sets foot on your property, set some rules in the contract. Will the workers be allowed to use your bathroom? Who will be in the house while they are working? Will they pay for extra heat and electricity consumed? If they tear up your yard will they repair it?

Contractors may take it personally if they're treated poorly. "There's an attitude against manual labor," says Richard Baronio, a New York City contractor. "People are ignorant and they get afraid and arrogant."

Being clear from the outset about your expectations and treating subcontractors like you'd want to be treated will set the right tone. "You want to establish a mutual relationship of trust and confidence," says McGinley of Peninsula Builders Exchange.

How Much Should You Pay, and How Can You Finance It?

If you're like most of us, you'll be tempted to go with the lowest offer you get for any project. Think again. Because of the fixed costs of material and labor, a contractor who offers you a stunningly low price is probably being deceptive, says Curtis, director of consumer affairs for the Denver, Colorado, district attorney's office. How does this scam work? Most common is the contractor who starts with a bargain-basement price but tells the customer about midway through that the work is more complicated (and more expensive) than the contractor thought. Some contractors base lowball estimates on sub-quality materials and then offer the homeowner a clearly better window, for example, midway through the process and try to talk the homeowner into upgrading. "Ultimately, you will pay more than you would have with a reputable person who started off at a reasonably higher price," says Curtis.

Baronio, the New York City contractor, says that when he started out in the business his bids were always higher than those of rivals because he was bidding what he actually thought the job would cost. These days, he doesn't bid at all, but gives customers a range of costs instead. "Making your decision simply on the basis of money is the wrong approach," he says.

To line up financing for your project, you'll want to get a sense of what the second-floor addition will cost. *Remodeling* magazine (www.remodelingmagazine.com) can help you eyeball costs, and even has average costs by project and by region.

Managing the Contractor

To understand how to manage the process of getting your dream remodeling accomplished, you need to know a little bit about how most contractors work. It's no secret that construction work is seasonal. Most contractors and their crews begin to get calls from homeowners for projects in the early spring, and the busy season gets underway in April in most parts of the country. And this has big implications for you: Your project will likely be just one of many crowding your contractor's list. With the contractor's attention divided, it's up to you to keep your project at the top of the list.

"Small contractors, when they get busy, are often not very good at paying attention to stuff. They don't schedule well. They have problems controlling people who work for them. You need to be a squeaky wheel," says Tom McGinley of Peninsula Builders Exchange. How to control the situation? McGinley suggests a formalized weekly meeting, either in person or on the phone, where you exchange information and questions with the contractor. Designate one family decision maker to talk to the contractor, and make sure that person is always talking directly to the contractor, not a site supervisor or subcontractor. Ask for work schedules, keeping in mind that each step in the construction process has a certain duration—for example, installing electrical systems, roofing—and many of these overlap. "It's not a linear process," McGinley says. "You can paint the interior while stuccoing the exterior." Keeping on top of where the contractor is in the process, though, will help keep the contractor focused on your job as well.

If you are really committed to making sure you're bringing your project in on time and on budget, try to keep yourself from making big changes in the plans. "When you make changes it disrupts the contractor's scheduling—and it makes the thing cost more," says McGinley. "Homeowners aren't used to that. Not being ready to pick the paint color can delay the whole project two weeks."

Nobody knows this lesson better than McGinley himself. When the contractor was adding a room to his own home, his wife decided in the middle of the project that she wanted to add a steam-generating machine to the bathroom shower he was building. No problem, thought McGinley, and he quickly located $1,000 worth of equipment that would transform the traditional shower into a spa-like sauna. Installing the steamer he figured would cost $575. Then he found a hitch. The manufacturer required that the machine producing the steam have 12 inches of clearance on all sides, and that it couldn't sit more than 25 feet from the point of release. Unfortunately, no matter where McGinley set the machine in the bathroom he couldn't meet those restrictions. So he figured that the best solution would be to put the steam unit in the attic and thread the steam pipes through the ceiling. That required building a hatch and a platform. Things got even more complex when a building inspector said McGinley would have to add a disconnect switch and a new circuit to the home's electrical panel so that the steam unit would meet safety requirements. Since the electrician was already finished with his work, he had to be recalled at an additional cost of $400 and a week's time. But McGinley's problems weren't over yet. Two walls of his shower stall were glass and didn't reach to the ceiling. Because the sauna had to be enclosed, the contractor had to extend the walls, steam proof them with rubber, and then slope the ceiling so that condensing water would fall immediately to the shower floor. Total cost? $4,000. "That's how your money gets eaten up," says McGinley.

Watch Out for Environmental Problems

Even if you've lived in your home for years, you may have problems that never get discovered until you make a major change like an addition. Imagine: A contractor comes into your home to replace those ugly acoustic tiles that have covered the rec room ceiling for 20 years. Early into the job he realizes that the tiles contain asbestos. If he's a responsible professional, he'll insist that the poisonous materials be taken out by a licensed asbestos removal contractor. This will take time and could ultimately cost you thousands of dollars. If he's less than honest, he'll ask for an extra few hundred bucks and offer to do the job himself. Even if the contractor doesn't make a mistake and release particles of cancer-causing dust into the air, he's still breaking the law, and the long-term repercussions are consequential.

Contractors who aren't licensed to deal with such materials can't dispose of them at licensed (and safe) facilities, says Ross Edward, a spokesman for the Massachusetts Department of Environmental Protection. And if hazardous materials aren't disposed of properly—say you've a leak in the pipe leading from your oil storage tank—they could leach into soil and groundwater. Scary, yes, and also illegal: If your contractor gets caught dumping, you may be liable since the pollution came from your property. "These days," says Edward, "the homeowner has just as much responsibility for the environment as any factory owner."

When Do You Know That Your Project Is Done?

Halfway into the construction process, you'll no doubt be dreaming of the day your project is over and the subcontractors take their muddy shoes and leave you in peace. "There's a point in the process where the customer wants to throw the towel in—finishes are still to be put in, everything is dusty and unfinished. They run out of faith," says New York contractor Baronio. And yet you'll no doubt be taken by surprise when your contractor informs you that he's packing up his tools because the job is done. How can he think about collecting his paycheck when the light fixtures aren't completely installed or maybe the garbage disposal isn't hooked up? "Most builders define a complete home as one that's ready for occupancy," says McGinley. "Usability is the key. From the owner's point of view, it's never completed." His suggestion? Don't make the final payment until the job is done, and if you expect perfection, specify it in your contract.

Another step you'll want to take once you agree the contractor has finished: Hire an inspector to give the new bedroom or basement game room a thorough once-over. The House Inspector's Tom Pendleton says that while builders have to adhere to local building codes, those specifications are minimal requirements only. Three years ago, he inspected a newly built family room addition to find that the floor sloped three inches from one end of the room to the other. It was a problem, but the mistake didn't violate local building regulations. "There are so many things the codes don't cover," he says. "There is no code for an uneven floor in your addition." The homeowner was able to recoup some of the monies needed for repair—largely because of having hired a home inspector to take a look at it.

Avoiding the "Re-muddle"

If you're considering a major change to your house, say, a second-story addition, you'll want to think long and hard about design changes. Sal Alfano, editor of *Remodeling* magazine, says some people who rush the process can end up with a "re-muddle" rather than a remodel. "They mix styles, or the proportions are wrong. It sticks out like a sore thumb on your block."

Before he even considers taking on a new project, Doug Walter, a Denver architect who specializes in designing additions, sits his client down, and the two evaluate whether they're using the existing house to the fullest extent possible. For example, a young couple recently approached him with the idea of building a great room onto their tiny two-bedroom bungalow. But Walter quickly determined that they never used a formal living room, largely because it was stuffed full of formal furniture. He suggested furnishing the room with more comfortable furniture (including a coffee table you could put your feet on) and then refinishing the basement, instead of building a great room. "You have to make every square foot work for you before you even think about an addition," he says.

How can you make sure that your project is a winner, not a candidate for the pages of *Lesser Homes and Gardens*? "Make sure your addition matches your original house. That means you want to match materials, the roof type and slope. Copy details," says Walter, who started his career in building preservation. (See Figure 6.1.) "You want the same type of windows in the same general arrangement. It's not just putting a box on top of or beside a house. You have to imagine how the original architect would have done it. A bad addition is risky at resale—it's like a bloody nose for the house. It's something that is obvious to everyone and decreases curb appeal. You won't get your in-

(*a*)

FIGURE 6.1   Remodel Before (*a*) and After (*b*)
Source: Copyright © 2003 by Doug Walter Architects.

vestment back, dollar for dollar, if people don't consider it as good a quality as the main house."

Most remodeling companies have a professional designer on staff or they may partner with architects, says Alfano. But if you hire an outside architect, don't let her fly solo. Involve the builder in the building design so you'll know ahead of time whether or not your architect's flights of fancy can be accomplished within your budget.

The most popular targets of remodeling work? Kitchens and bathrooms. "That's what the homeowners value most," says Harvard's Kermit Baker. It's also where homeowners spend most of their time, and because of that these two rooms reflect the changing lifestyles of homeowners. In the late 1980s and early 1990s, kitchens were typically next to the family room so that moms could watch kids while they cooked. And as homes have gotten bigger to accommodate those families, so, too, have the number of bathrooms increased. The average new home built today has two-and-a-half or three bathrooms.

(b)

FIGURE 6.1   (Continued)

But as the population ages, remodeling dollars are starting to go to other parts of the house. Master bedrooms are being expanded to include elaborate baths and even miniature kitchens. Some homes are being designed so their owners can stay put well into their elderly years with broader doors to accommodate wheelchairs, first-floor master bedrooms, and easy-to-open catches rather than doorknobs. Ultimately, your project must answer the needs of your own situation, whether it's an expanding family or simply a desire for more space. But you'll also want to keep in mind whether the changes you're making today will appeal to potential buyers down the road.

One of the easiest homes to extensively remodel, says Walter, is the old-fashioned ranch. Many of the homes built in this design style in the 1950s and 1960s were constructed with inexpensive materials, such as bargain molding and single-pane aluminum windows. "What we do with those homes is give them more quality—replace all hollow core doors with paneled doors," he says. "We replace the windows, upgrade the mechanical systems, including plumbing and electrical. We redo counters in kitchens."

Watch out for this common mistake made by first timers: overbuilding. "It's pretty easy to remodel yourself out of your neighborhood," says Alfano. "Be aware of house values around you. If you spend 50 percent of what you paid for a house on a remodeling project, you won't get that money back if you sell your house in a year. In a faster-growth market, you get your value back faster."

7

MANAGING
YOUR INVESTMENT

Major renovation projects are a great way to keep your home's value from plunging. But there are many other steps you'll need to take between major projects to keep your home in good condition. Regular maintenance can prevent many of the worst-case scenarios that can rob your house of value and resale appeal. In this chapter, we'll look at how you can protect your family and your home, reducing the possibility of disasters like mold infestations, but also lessening the likelihood that you'll fall victim to home pollutants that can be just as devastating. (You thought radon was bad? Wait until you see the evil that lurks in the range hood of your professional oven.) We'll give you solid advice on how to get a home insurance policy that won't land you in the poorhouse. And, if your insurer is refusing to cover the damage from the time your gas grill morphed into a small inferno, well, we've got advice for that, too.

Is Your House Killing You?

Ask new homeowners how they spend their time and you're likely to get an exhausted look in response. That's because after months of searching for just the right house and weeks of closing the deal, new homeowners normally spend a lot of time fixing things up, making the new place suitable for their family. There's the gas grill to install outside, or repainting the baby's room. Unfortunately, too much time is spent on superficial improvements, and way too little effort is spent on learning the home's major systems, the plumbing, electrical, heating, and even roof and outdoor sheathing that will have to be looked after for as long as you own your home. No doubt you've gotten some clue how your home's mechanical systems work from your inspection at the time of purchase, but that's just a start, says Tom Greiner, an associate professor at Iowa State University.

Begin, he says, with the furnace. Most homeowners are told that the only check they need to make of their home's heating system (if it's a gas furnace) each year is a peek inside to make sure the flame is burning blue, to indicate it's not producing carbon monoxide. Not true, says Greiner. Owners should actually hire an inspector each fall to run their furnace through its paces. A professional, he says, will cycle the furnace off and on to make sure it lights evenly, and will also measure the draft and make sure there is sufficient airflow going into the system. "Otherwise," says Greiner, "you'd be breathing fumes coming off that ignition."

Remember, many older furnaces require air from outside to operate correctly. When basements are sealed tight with caulk and sealant, the furnace may not be able to draw in air as it should. And that breathing has to go on throughout a cold winter's day as your furnace turns off and on to regulate temperature. A qualified heating contractor can also check to make sure the vent and chimney system is working without a hitch, transporting corrosive gases out of the house efficiently. If the furnace doesn't vent properly, carbon monoxide can build up, a dangerous situation that leads to hundreds of deaths every year. Greiner advises installing carbon monoxide alarms on every floor in your home where people sleep. "This is something you need to be concerned about," he says.

If you've recently purchased a home, no doubt you've also had both your electrical system and the plumbing inspected. But there are things you'll want to watch out for. You'll know there are problems with the electrical system if circuit breakers are tripping, or if you smell hot wiring or see a flickering of lights. Watch out, too, for warm plugs. Any of these can be a sign of problems that could lead to an electrical fire.

Keep an eye out for leaking plumbing as well. If your water pump is running frequently or your water bills are high, you may have a problem. Standing water is an open invitation to creeping crud—toxic molds—which can quickly infest your home, ruining your investment and your health (more about mold later in this chapter). If your water comes from a well, have it inspected each year or after any flooding, which can result in well water contamination. If your home has a septic tank, forget the conventional wisdom that it doesn't need maintenance. Greiner suggests an inspection each and every year to check the build up of waste material. Most new septic tanks have access holes that allow homeowners to check those levels on their own. Think such checks are optional? Imagine the trouble if the septic tank backs up in the winter when cold lines could trap waste material, forcing it to back up inside your house.

Roofs may have a 20- to 30-year life, but you'll want to get up on your roof every year for a quick inspection and to clean out the gutters. Look for missing or curled shingles, which suggest that your roofing is nearing the end of its life. Gutters should drain 5 to 10 feet away from the house, and your yard should naturally slope away from the house, allowing rainwater to drain away from your basement. Water buildup is a major cause of basement cracking and failing. Consider relandscaping your yard if rainwater isn't draining properly, but make sure that any dirt brought in is at least eight inches away from the home's foundation (otherwise, you risk rotting the exterior siding).

What many homeowners don't consider is the fact that these major systems interact with each other in sometimes unpredictable ways. For example, if, like a lot of people, you've purchased one of the popular professional-style ovens for your kitchen that has an oversized range hood and exhaust fan, you'll want to keep your eyes peeled for what engineers call "backdrafting." What can happen, especially in homes that were built tight to promote energy efficiency, is that the exhaust fan in the kitchen can create a sucking action that actually pulls the very fumes your house is trying to expel, like the furnace emissions or smoke from the fireplace, back into the house. Consult a qualified heating contractor to make sure this isn't happening in your home.

Even your attached garage can create unexpected problems, says Greiner. "What we are finding is that air flows from the garage into the house, especially in winter. Warm air from inside the home leaks out the roof, and that sucks the air in from the garage." That means fumes given off by anything stored in the garage, such as fertilizer, chemicals, and pesticides, can sneak into the house. Store such materials outside if your garage is attached. You might also want to think twice about leaving your car running for a long period inside the garage to heat it up on cold mornings.

The Mold Threat

Beverly Hammond knew something was wrong just before Thanksgiving 2001. That's when she went to her foyer closet to pull out a leaf for the dining room table. No sooner had she opened the door than she smelled a strange odor. Then she saw it—a black, gooey mold coating the table leaf, as well as a rolled-up carpet leaning against it.

"My heart sank," she remembers. After extensive testing, the Hammonds discovered that their suburban Houston house hosted a virulent toxic mold that had crept from a bathroom throughout the house. The fungus even sandwiched itself between the wallpaper and the walls. Hammond suspects that the mold was responsible for her own health problems and those of her husband. Both had been diagnosed with chronic fatigue, which means they tire easily and suffer from mysterious rashes and joint pains.

After reporting the mold to their insurer, the family wrapped up the affected areas with plastic wrap to keep it from spreading and moved into tents in their backyard. Ten months later (and still living in tents), the Hammonds finally started getting the insurance money they needed to rid the house of the toxic mold. They believe their insurer has dragged out the process to pay as little as possible in the cleanup. "There are nights I cry and can't sleep," Hammond says.

Mold has been around forever (methods for mold cleanup are described in the Bible), but until recently it didn't figure much into the lives of most homeowners. While mold spores are common, they tend to collect and grow only when exposed to water, such as in a shower stall or wet basement. But an escalation of mold reports leads some to contend there's more than just a few leaky basements to blame. Some people believe that new construction methods that seal homes tight to promote energy efficiency have increased the number of homes contaminated with mold. They say that the lack of air moving through walls means moisture gets trapped inside, allowing fungi to feast on drywall. But the truth is there is no consensus on why or even whether mold is a bigger problem now than it was previously.

By one measure, though, mold is big. The nation's insurers paid out $1.3 billion in claims due to mold in 2001, up from negligible amounts just two years earlier, says Robert Hartwig, chief economist at the Insurance Information Institute. Insurers are working to reduce those payouts. Hartwig says that insurers in every state have asked regulators to exclude mold from the list of items that insurers have to cover, and many large insurers are announcing they won't cover it at all. Meanwhile, rising mold claims are pushing premiums and rates higher. In 2002, rates were expected to rise 9 to 10 percent largely because of mold claims, Hartwig says.

Not all mold develops into the kind of problem faced by the Hammonds. In fact, mold spores waft through just about every household. It's only when they land on damp spots and find a food source, such as wood, paper, or carpet, that they blossom. Worse than the home damage, though, can be the health consequences. David Straus, professor of microbiology and immunology at Texas Tech University, has studied mold for nine years, and says it's clear that exposure to mold inside buildings is detrimental to human health, and can cause everything from hay fever and inflammation of the lungs to asthma and fungal infections.

The best way to keep your home free of mold is to attend to plumbing and roof leaks immediately. Standing water is an open invitation to mold spores to collect and reproduce. Maintain indoor humidity levels at 30 to 60 percent. Make sure the house is ventilated—even out-of-the-way corners need circulating air (think the Hammonds' foyer closet). Small mold problems, especially those on hard surfaces, can be cleaned simply with soap and water. If mold attacks spongy surfaces, such as carpets or even drywall, your best bet is to remove the materials from your home entirely. Extensive mold problems will have to be handled by experts, usually called remediators, who undertake the most radical tactics in combating mold, stripping rooms down to the studs on the walls. (This isn't, by the way, something you want to try on your own, since moving mold can cause more spores to become airborne and infect other parts of your house.)

If you're buying a home, keep an eye out for these signals that a mold problem has developed: discoloration of ceiling tiles or sheetrock, evidence of flooding in the basement, warped baseboards. Remember, because mold can form in hard-to-spot places, like behind walls and underneath vinyl wallpaper, a strong musty odor throughout a house should be a warning sign to buyers.

Don't think that mold affects homes only in lowland areas. "There's not one state that's not represented in our database," says Melinda Ballard, who started the Policyholders of America (POA) web site, (www.policyholdersofamerica.org) after her own 12,000-square-foot Dripping Springs, Texas, mansion was overtaken by Stachybotrys, a particularly virulent mold. Her own story shows the importance of acting quickly to combat mold problems. Her insurer's investigation of the family's complaints about mold went on for two years. During that time, the Ballards were told not to take action to stop the problem. As a result, the mold crept throughout the house, overtaking much of it in just two months. A jury ordered the Ballards' home insurer to pay $32 million after determining that the insurer failed to rectify the problem. That decision is currently being appealed. (See Sidebar 7.1.)

Fighting Back

If your home insurer is refusing to pay all or part of a claim, you can fight back and win. The trick is to follow a few simple steps.

Your first line of defense is to document everything. If your home is damaged and you decide to make a claim, get written copies of police or fire department reports, and of appraisals made by outsiders. Consider this ammunition, so you can prove your claim is legitimate.

If a claim is challenged, complain to your insurer first, and don't take the first negative answer as final. Make it clear that you'll go to your state's insurance regulators if you're not given your say. (To get the telephone number of your state's insurance department, log on to the National Association of Insurance Commissioners web site at www.naic.org.) "Many states publicize each company's complaint record, and sometimes companies will act appropriately to avoid embarrassment," says Douglas Heller of the Foundation for Taxpayer & Consumer Rights in Los Angeles. Heller adds one caveat: Many home and auto policies impose a one-year time limit on legal challenges to claim decisions—and the clock starts ticking as soon as the first decision is made. If you don't have an answer within a month of your complaint, it's time to go to the state.

Once your state regulator looks into your complaint, insurers usually have six weeks to resolve the dispute. Unfortunately, unless your insurer broke the law, most state regulators lack the authority to enforce a resolution. The only avenue left is a lawsuit, and that's seldom worthwhile. Contingency-fee attorneys—who get paid only if you win—take on insurance cases. But if the disagreement with your insurer is over just a couple of thousand dollars, even a contingency-fee lawyer may not deem your case worthy of his or her time. Your best bet? Find a new insurer.

Insuring Your Home

You may not be able to insure your home against the threat of mold—for now—but there are plenty of other potential disasters you can protect yourself from, such as fire, theft, and the like. Unfortunately, getting coverage for your castle isn't as cheap as it was even a couple of years ago. The insurance industry has been squeezed by bigger-than-expected losses and the bear market. As a result, the industry is squeezing its customers right back. Premiums for home coverage were expected to rise 9 percent in 2003, leaving the average household paying 21 percent more for homeowner's insurance than it did in 2000. And carriers have slapped customers with double- and even triple-digit rate hikes this year. AT&T retiree Art Roy paid State Farm $994 in 2002 for $104,000 in coverage on his ranch-style house near Dallas. That's 45 percent more than he paid the previous year—and his rates would have gone up 104 percent if he hadn't agreed to reduced coverage for drapes, carpets, and clothing.

Rising premiums aren't the only problem for insurance shoppers. Carriers have become more sophisticated about identifying people who are likely to file claims and cost them a bundle. While you may feel you're the safest customer to ever step into an agent's office, your insurer may think otherwise. Common sense says your home's value ought to determine the amount of premium you pay, but that's no longer the underwriter's chief concern. Insurers now base many of their underwriting decisions on everything from your credit history to your Chihuahua's bad temper—judgments that can send your premiums spiraling or deny you coverage altogether.

What's going to slash your premiums? Patience and a good road map. We'll show you how to shop shrewdly for home insurance and how to fight your insurer if one of your claims is rejected. We've also got some top-rate online references to help you make the right decisions about your coverage.

First off, you're going to need a policy that will replace your home and your possessions, down to the last theme-park tchotchke, and provide liability coverage if someone gets hurt on your property. To protect your home and possessions, go for replacement-cost coverage, which pays you the policy's face value—the amount of money it would cost to rebuild your home if it were totally destroyed. (The alternative is cash-value coverage, which pays you the loss of the value of your property, minus depreciation.)

It's crucial that you know how much it would cost to replace your home before you shop for coverage. To estimate the replacement cost, calculate how many square feet are in your house and multiply that figure by the local construction cost per square foot for homes that are similar to yours. Some insurance web sites, like InsWeb (www.insweb.com), offer free cost calculators.

Whatever you do, don't underestimate the value of your belongings. The maximum coverage you can get for your possessions on most policies equals 75 percent of the replacement cost of your house. That's usually enough for most folks, but if your Aunt Pauline's sable coat is nesting comfortably in your closet, you may need to pay extra to insure it. The same may be true for art, antiques, jewelry, and your personal computer system, which are each insured for no more than $5,000 on most policies. You can buy additional coverage on these heirlooms for relatively little; most insurers charge 25 cents to $1.50 for every additional $100 of protection. (See Sidebar 7.2.)

Your homeowner's policy typically includes between $100,000 and $300,000 of liability coverage, which can come in especially handy if you have children. Let's say your teenage daughter accidentally knocks someone silly at the ice-skating rink; your homeowner's coverage will pay the victim's medical expenses and foot your legal bills should the mishap spill over into court. But if you own a car and a home, you should invest in umbrella coverage, which provides at least $1 million in additional liability protection beyond what you have with your auto and home policies. Umbrella policies cover you and your family in virtually any wrongdoing, from libel and slander accusations to charges stemming from a playground fight. (One person who benefited from an umbrella liability policy: President Bill Clinton, who used his coverage to pay part of his settlement in the Paula Jones ruckus.)

Now that you know what type and how much coverage you need, it's time to find the best possible deal. Most insurance is sold through three channels: national carriers such as State Farm and Allstate, inde-

What Does Your Coverage Really Cover?

It's the ultimate homeowner nightmare: A house fire that consumes not only your home but your possessions—the photo albums and grade school report cards—as well. The unthinkable happened one cold February evening to Penni and Richard Domikis. Richard discovered it coming home to their rural Fredericksburg, Virginia, log cabin home from his job as an engineer in Washington, D.C. In no time at all, the whole house was a loss—some $250,000 up in smoke. The good news? Neither Penni nor their son Noah, who had been out shopping, had been hurt.

A house burns every 82 seconds in the United States, and few events are more horrible. But the Domikises were in for a lesson: Things could get worse. The couple was devastated to learn that that their coverage would not be nearly enough to rebuild their ruined house and replace their possessions. For two years, the couple fought with their insurer Allstate over the settlement, hiring a lawyer and making an appeal to the state's insurance department.

Allstate maintained that it had notified the couple before the fire that it would no longer offer them full replacement coverage, saying it was only obligated to pay 120 percent of the assessed value of the home plus 75 percent of the assessed value to cover contents. But the Domikises said they were never adequately notified of the change in coverage. After the Virginia regulators started writing letters on the family's behalf, Allstate paid an additional $25,000 over the limits of the amended policy. But the couple figure that they still were out-of-pocket $200,000 for contents and $50,000 in construction costs.

"No matter how nice your agent is," Richard told *SmartMoney*, "you're dealing with a pool of lawyers when you lose your home."

What should homeowners do to make sure they don't get burned after a home fire?

- *Read your policy.* Sounds simple, but most homeowners stuff this document in a desk drawer, ignoring its fine print until a fire strikes. What happens? You get fried when trying to recoup your losses. You best protection: Discuss any renovations or major purchases with your agent, and make him or her show you—in writing—where they're covered in your policy. Also, be sure you read the notices that come with your monthly bill that will alert you to any policy changes.

- *Add more coverage where needed.* Even guaranteed replacement cost (generally the most extensive insurance) won't ensure total coverage. Say your wedding silverware, valued at about $5,000, gets destroyed in a fire. Fortunately, it's covered by your homeowner's insurance. Unfortunately, insurers may pay only up to $2,500 to have it replaced. For complete coverage, you'll need a $10 to $15 rider to your policy. The same goes for valuables like jewelry and stamp collections.

- *Keep up with the codes.* You fell in love with that turn-of-the-century farmhouse. Great. Just one thing: Make sure your policy covers the cost of complying with new building codes and ordinances when rebuilding. If local property setbacks are changed, some insurance plans won't cover the costs to comply with the revamped footprint. You can purchase an ordinance endorsement from your carrier, which will cover such an expense.

- *Don't get taken to the cleaners.* Your insurer will offer to have your possessions professionally cleaned. Don't let it happen until you're in agreement on the damages. Not only is cleaning smoke-damaged clothes or furniture expensive (up to $15,000 for a three-bedroom home), but you'll pay the fee. And there's no guarantee your sofa won't smell sooty. Douglas L. LaFaive, a Connecticut-based public adjuster, says humid weather will draw any embedded smell from your "cleaned" couch.

- *Get some help.* If you feel overwhelmed, contact a public adjuster. For a fee of 5 to 15 percent of the settlement, accredited public insurance adjusters will do the dirty work of reading the technical jargon and guiding you through the complicated claims process.

SIDEBAR 7.2

pendent agents, and direct sellers who let you buy policies by phone and over the Internet. Normally, the best deals can be found with the Big Three (State Farm, Allstate, and Farmers). But that's no longer true. With the pressure on for sales, even companies represented by high-commission independent agents, (Chubb, Hartford, or Travelers, among others) can be competitive.

To get an idea of just how much you'll pay, head to the Internet. Many state governments (28 states for auto insurance, 23 for home) post sample premiums from insurers online; they're usually sorted by county or town, letting you find the best prices in your area. You can find an index of web sites at www.naic.org, the home of the National Association of Insurance Commissioners. Keep in mind that these quotes won't match exactly what you'll eventually pay—they won't take your credit or claims history into account, for example—but they'll give you an idea of what to expect once you start working the phones.

As you contact companies for quotes, ask for any discounts that apply. Hanging with the right crowd can also cut your premiums. Many carriers offer attractive prices through professional groups or alumni associations. At Liberty Mutual, for example, graduates of 200 colleges can get discounts of up to 15 percent, on top of any other premium breaks for which they qualify.

There's a good chance that one of the companies that you contact will refer you to an independent agent to handle the sale. If not, contact one in your area anyway; he or she may be able to beat the quotes you got elsewhere. And an agent can also help you when there's something on your record that could make it tricky to buy insurance—so-so credit, for example, or a bad driving record—by steering you to companies that are willing to insure those kinds of records.

Insurers are becoming more forgiving of some of your transgressions, but they are cracking down on others. Carriers are so eager to cut their losses that it's best to pay for small home repairs yourself. If you don't, you could end up like Etsuko Suzuki, who started insuring her home in Seattle with Safeco in 1994. When a windstorm in 1999 knocked down her fence, Safeco paid for the repairs. And when sparks escaping from her grill charred a small section of her deck, Safeco paid to fix that, too. But then she got a letter of cancellation from Safeco, saying that two claims in one year was too high a risk for the company to renew her contract. "If I'd known they were going to drop me, I wouldn't [have made the claims]."

Suzuki did get new coverage, but because the insurers consider her a "substandard risk," her premiums skyrocketed and she found many companies would not insure her at all. Her costs tripled—her premiums are now $1,500 a year, and that's with a $2,500 deductible.

As you start shopping to insure your home, it's crucial that you have a clear sense of what you need—and refuse to let your insurer make that call for you. Trudi and Keith Hall were infuriated when their insurer boosted the value of their house in Mobile, Alabama. When their home-insurance renewal notice came one summer from Travelers, they found their premium had been hiked almost 40 percent, to $1,397. (Later it was jacked up to $1,800.) Trudi's agent told her that a Travelers adjuster had blown up her policy with a "drive-by appraisal." Without entering the property, the adjuster eyeballed the house and figured that it would cost some $225,000 to rebuild—including $20,300 to rebuild "other structures" on the Halls' property. The Halls have only one "other structure": a swing set. "My five kids are real excited to see what kind of swings they can get for twenty grand," Trudi mused at the time. Travelers told the Halls there was nothing they could do about the appraisal—so they shopped around for another policy, ultimately buying a $950 policy from Allstate. "People tend to get jerked around because they get intimidated," says Trudi, who located the new policy through an agent she found on the Web. "Consumers should rule."

When you check out a homeowner's policy, be leery of the footnotes attached. To be covered in a flood, you have to buy a separate policy from the federally supervised National Flood Insurance Program (800-427-4661). The average policyholder pays about $350 a year for $125,000 worth of coverage, but the policies aren't quite that simple. For you to get a nickel from the policy, the flood has to damage two adjacent properties. Regardless of how big the flood, the policies never pay for damages to family heirlooms stored in a basement.

Even if you live in an area prone to tremblors, earthquake coverage usually isn't worth the cost. If you live in California, your policy will typically carry a 15 percent deductible on the replacement cost of your house for earthquake damages. That means you won't see a penny from your insurer until you spend tens of thousands on repairs, a threshold you'll reach only in a major earthquake. When a tremblor measuring 5.2 on the Richter scale shook Napa Valley a few years ago, 2,800 people had earthquake insurance but fewer than 10 percent had claims that were large enough to get any money back.

There's no substitute for knowing exactly what it is you're buying. Not only will it help to keep you from overpaying, it will help you get the most out of what you buy. When Lisa Lauenberg bought her condo in Kirkland, Washington, she knew enough to trim her homeowner's premium by asking for a home-and-auto discount. Her new home also put her less than a mile from her job at a paging company, so she lobbied hard and got a discount for drivers with short commutes. "Hey," she told *SmartMoney* magazine, "you have to be persistent to get what you want." You can't argue with the payoff: Lauenberg shaved $250 a year—more than 25 percent—off her premium.

Insurance for Your Investment

Getting coverage for your investment property was never easy, but the terrorist attacks of September 11, 2001, a rash of subsequent weather and fire disasters, plus mold hysteria drove rates for commercial coverage up by about 30 percent in 2002 alone, says P. J. Crowley, vice president of the New York City–based Insurance Information Institute (www.iii.org). Already, the rates for rental property were about 25 percent higher than for primary residences, according to independent agent Charlie Nusbaum, president of S. L. Nusbaum Insurance in Norfolk, Virginia. "Owners have a bigger incentive to maintain a property than renters," says Crowley. "If you own a home and live in it, you're more attentive to the little problems that can build into big problems."

Worse, many insurance firms are shying away from covering rental properties at all. "This issue is taking a lot of people by surprise," says Fred Prassas, vice president of the Institute of Real Estate

Management. "When they're closing on a place, people are calling their insurance agents and getting the scary shock that they might not be able to do it right now."

For that reason, before you close on a home, you'll want to get your hands on something called a Comprehensive Loss Underwriting Exchange (CLUE) report, which details the home's insurance claim history. "If it has a clean insurance record, it's a house that has been well maintained," says Crowley. "If it has a history of water damage claims, you should know it before you buy it." Unfortunately, you won't be able to order one of these reports on your own when you're shopping around for different properties. The best thing to do is to require a CLUE report as a condition of sale.

Another step you'll want to take to keep your insurance bill down to a manageable size is to increase your deductible. According to State Farm, going with an $800 deductible instead of a $500 deductible on a $200,000 policy could save you $70 annually. Hiring a property manager may also allow you to lower your premiums, especially if you live out of state. Requiring your tenants to carry their own apartment insurance can cut your bill, too. Make sure you shop your current insurer—the one who writes your personal coverage for your home or car—first.

Once you buy, keep tabs on what your tenants are up to. Illinois landlord Allen Bailey was alarmed when he drove by one of his purchases in little Metropolis, along the Ohio River, and saw a sign for "Aloha Pools" in the front yard. Since the place didn't have a pool when he rented it out, Bailey's jaw dropped. "The worst scenario is if someone drowned in that pool," says Bailey. "And then the family could sue for millions." He had the tenants sign new papers, taking responsibility for the costs of the pool and whatever happened in it.

8

How to Get Your Ideal Second Home

I magine buying a home that hugs the shoreline, or one that graces the top of the mountain. Sounds great, doesn't it? According to the National Association of Realtors, which surveys second homes sales every other year, 359,000 such sales were completed in 2001, off 1999's blistering pace due to the recession, but still the second highest sales total since 1989. What's more, buyers are paying more than ever before for their vacation abodes. Median prices in 2001 skyrocketed 26.8 percent to $162,000—that's up from $127,800 in 1999 and higher than the median price for primary homes.

If you're like many recent second-home shoppers, though, you'll expect your vacation home to do double duty—that is, serving as a weekend getaway at first and then ultimately as your retirement home. Like Bob Will. When he spoke to *SmartMoney* magazine, the geophysicist had spent the past couple of decades knocking himself out: long hours, intense pressure on the job, loads of business travel dragging him away from his family for weeks. It had taken a toll, and the then 43-year-old boomer wanted nothing more than a nice, comfortable, and early retirement.

He could picture it perfectly: He'd drop out of the corporate world and head for New Mexico, where he went to college. Maybe he'd do a little consulting work, but mainly he'd relax. Do some hunting. Go hiking. Ski. Luxuriate in the clean, fresh air.

There was only one problem with this daydream: money. Housing prices in Santa Fe had skyrocketed in the prior few years, and as far as Will could see they would only keep going up. How was he ever going to afford this, especially on what he assumed would be a sharply reduced income?

Will's solution: He bought his retirement home way ahead of time, while he was still earning a full-time wage. The three-bedroom house in Taos, a charming and spectacularly scenic town about an hour's drive from Santa Fe, cost only 40 percent of what he would have paid south in Santa Fe.

"I was shocked at the values I could get in Taos," Will said. "It's the world's best-kept secret." And here's the best part: He rented out the house for about $800 a month, so it's very nearly paying for itself until he's ready to retire. It's great," he said. "Every day, every week, I'm building equity in a comfortable retirement. It's gratifying to have taken care of this."

It's not always so easy to turn a dream into retirement gold, but in this chapter we'll help you find your own second home property that can double as a retirement home. We'll take a look at the vacation communities that are emerging as new destinations for retirees. Want to know whether you can swing financing a vacation home now? We'll show you how your banker will analyze a second home mortgage application. Plus, you'll learn the intricacies of second home tax planning and how to hire a property manager.

Where to Buy

It used to be that if you were buying a second home for retirement, there were only a few places that would naturally spring to mind: the retirement enclaves of Florida's east and west coasts or maybe the golf-course-pocked deserts of Arizona. These days, though, you're really only limited by your imagination. Take Ashland, Oregon. Just 15 miles from the border of California, this little burg is not the first place you'd think of to spend your golden years. But Rad Welles, an agent at Lithia Realty, says that over 50 percent of the town's population are retired or semiretired. "They're an older, moneyed crowd who originally came here to see the plays," says Welles, referring to the town's summer Shakespeare festival that draws thousands of visitors each year. But once they visited, they were hooked by the area's small-town charm and physical beauty.

The attraction of Avalon, a town on New Jersey's Seven Mile barrier island, is pretty uncomplicated: beachfront and plenty of it. Because of the town's proximity to the major population centers of Manhattan and Philadelphia, it has attracted a big following that has pushed prices skyward. Real estate agent Ralph Tiz says average home prices in Avalon are $900,000, and that investors are drawn to the area because of its consistent 10 percent year-to-year growth in prices.

To be sure, the range of possible locations for second homes is huge. But if you're choosing a spot with an eye toward its ultimate value as well as making sure it fits your family's needs, what's the best place for you and your significant other to target?

Charles F. Longino Jr. has a few ideas. A professor at Wake Forest University, Longino is one of the nation's most preeminent experts on retiree migration. He says that the states that traditionally have led in attracting retirees—Florida, California, New Jersey, and New York—are losing some of their edge. Take the Sunshine State. Between 1985 and 1990, Florida received nearly a quarter—23.8 percent—of all older migrants. Since 1960, it had led other states in attracting retirees, but between 1980 and 1990 Florida lost a 2 percent share of retirees (even though the numbers continued to rise). The other leading states experienced the same kinds of market share erosion. California, for example, has been ranked the number two draw for retirees since 1960, but its share of retirees has declined in every decade since that time, from 13.6 percent to 6.9 percent, according to Longino.

What's going on? Well, some of these states would appear to have fewer of the qualities that attracted retirees in the first place: low crime rates, good nearby hospitals, low cost of living, low housing costs, and friendly neighbors. While many of the original attractions—like mild climate—still exist, some older traditional retirement communities have matured into, well, cities with all the same problems people faced back home.

What do these past migration patterns have to do with your decision to buy a vacation home today? Well, if you are shopping for a vacation house that can make the transition into a retirement home, you'll want to examine the community for its fit as you age. Will it have the kind of atmosphere that will appeal to you when you are 75, rather than 45? Are costs reasonable, or are you selecting a high-tax, high-cost region that will bleed money from your retirement nest egg? Does the remote, lakeside home you've chosen happen to be located hours from any medical facilities? As you move into retirement, is the home located near work centers where you can gain a part-time income? Do the recreational amenities suit your tastes? (See Sidebar 8.1.)

The way the boomers answer these questions over the coming years—2008 is when they start retiring en masse—will determine the hot new retirement communities of the future. In other words, anticipate the boomers and you could be in on the ground floor of the next Sun Valley or Miami. One surprising choice is already emerging. "In the 1990s, rural areas in the U.S. grew through migration from metro areas," says Kenneth Johnson, a professor of sociology at the Loyola University in Chicago. "It's only the second time in the last 80 or 90 years that they've grown to that extent." What's going on? Johnson believes that a new generation of soon-to-be-retirees is choosing rural areas near their primary homes over more traditional locales. This Lake Wobegon trend allows them to disengage from the workforce slowly, and for that reason settlement is already starting in rural areas that border bigger cities like Boston and Manhattan. "You can't be way out in the Adirondacks if you have to be back in town for work Monday and Tuesday," he says.

Locating close in has other advantages, too. Consider Wisconsin's Walworth County, just north of Chicago. At one time, this area was known as a stomping ground for the Midwestern city's elite, whose mansions lined Lake Geneva. "Wealthy Chicagoans had their homes

Where to Buy the Vacation House You'll Retire To

Looking for a second home locale that can pull double duty as vacation getaway and retirement enclave? Consider these 10 affordable and attractive destinations.

Hendersonville, North Carolina. Due to the mild climate in the Blue Ridge Mountain valley, Carolina residents have been retiring here in western North Carolina since the days before air-conditioning. But this small, heavily forested town has been overshadowed of late by nearby Asheville, which has been touted by the AARP—so there's still plenty of room. Outdoor lures include hiking and canoeing. Indoors, the town boasts the State Theater and a Hendersonville Philharmonic. Health care is excellent, between the town's own hospital and the specialized care in Asheville. And a three-bedroom, two-bath house averages just $160,000; only 3 percent of homes here run more than $350,000.

Gadsden, Alabama. Golf heaven: There are eight courses nearby, and one of them is part of the renowned Robert Trent Jones Golf Trail (eight linked courses), which boasts PGA and LPGA tournament venues. Tucked in Alabama's Northern Highlands, Gadsden is a small town just a couple of hours from Birmingham and Atlanta. Costs of living and housing are low: A new three-bedroom brick house costs around $130,000.

Ithaca, New York. Some retirees are forsaking the Sun Belt for four-season living; those who don't mind a serious winter might want to call this college town home. Cornell University (and Ithaca College) bring culture and superb health care to the community. Nearly 10 percent of the population is over 65, so retirees will be in good company yet not have to worry about feeling as if they live in an old folks' home. There's a small airport in town for visitors and getaways. Three-bedroom, two-bath houses range from $125,000 to $200,000.

Boulder City, Nevada. Las Vegas is rolling out across the Nevada desert, absorbing everything in its path. But Boulder City, 25 miles away, purchased 167 square miles of desert south and west of town, blocking Vegas's sprawl and banning all development for the foreseeable future. Gambling is not permitted, and unlike other desert communities, Boulder City has an oasis: A part of town overlooks Lake Mead. Custom-built homes with a view of the lake cost over $300,000, but a similar one in town, with a pool, will run closer to $200,000.

Sequim, Washington. There's no denying the Pacific Northwest's gorgeous scenery, nor its heavy, depressing rainfall. Luckily, Sequim (pronounced "skwim") sits in the shadow of the Olympic Mountains, so it gets only 16 inches of rain per year. (In Seattle, you can expect double that.) Sequim has ocean straits to the north, mountains to the south; you can bike, hike, kayak, or go salmon fishing in Olympic National Park. New three-bedroom, two-bath homes sell for about $170,000.

Sandpoint, Idaho. If you missed buying in Aspen or Steamboat Springs, where prices have gotten unspeakable over the past 15 years, consider this ski area 50 miles from the Canadian border. Sandpoint sits amid the Selkirk and Cabinet mountains, but it's not just another Swiss Miss copy of the Alps. Come year-round to swim, fish, and sail on the Pend Oreille Lake (140 square miles) and River. Deluxe mountain cabins run about $200,000, but a newer ski chalet or a ranch house on the water costs at least $300,000.

Hatteras Island, North Carolina. Finding ocean property on any U.S. coastline—without spending a fortune—requires some roadwork. Luckily, you can still buy an affordable modern saltbox in one of the seven small villages on this quaint island. There's surfing, fishing, kayaking, and the 3,000-acre Buxton Woods for hiking or horseback riding. Vacation-home management consultant George Volsky says northern towns such as Waves or Rodanthe will be developers' next target. Few waterfront lots are left, but a three-bedroom house five minutes' walk from the beach can be had for under $300,000.

Phoenicia, New York. Woodstock is pricey, and the crowds have worn its bohemian atmosphere pretty thin. This little Catskill Mountains burg 20 miles away is a lot more mellow. Nearby attractions include historic Colonial-era homes and the Hudson River. There's skiing at Belleayre and Hunter mountains, and tubing at the Esopus Creek in the summer. Phoenicia is only two hours from New York City. Cabin-style homes begin at $150,000; more luxurious chalets and contemporaries start at $300,000.

Blue Ridge, Georgia. Instead of going down to overcrowded Orlando or the Florida Keys, some folks from Atlanta are heading to North Georgia. Why is this town a choice retreat? No worries about overdevelopment—42 percent of Fannin County is owned by the National Forest Service. After hiking the Appalachian mountain trails, head to the 100-year-old downtown to furnish your new house at the antiques stores and galleries. Two-bedroom cabins in the woods start at $150,000. Prices climb to over $400,000 for a house on several acres or for one closer to the river or Blue Ridge Lake.

Michigan City, Indiana. With record-setting prices for lakefront property just across the Michigan state border, this old Lake Michigan port is looking better and better. Just one hour and change from the Loop in downtown Chicago, Michigan City offers houses with views of the lake starting at $375,000. Local attractions range from an art museum and the Blue Chip Casino to major-league outlet shopping. The primary draw: barefooting on Lake Michigan's beaches.

there," says Johnson. There were homes belonging to the scions of Chicago—the Swifts, the Montgomery Wards, and the Searses. Today, the place is teeming with middle-class folks buying second homes close enough to their primary homes that they can drive there quickly. "People tell you, 'We're thinking of retiring here because our children are nearby and we want to see our grandchildren grow up,' " he says.

And it's not just Walworth County. Other rural communities that are beginning to grow include Wolfe County, Kentucky, which is far enough away from the more citified Lexington to be attractive, but convenient to reach because of a four-lane highway. Washington, D.C., residents are snapping up property in rural Clarke County, Virginia. In short, it's difficult to find a major metropolitan area that isn't spawning some sort of new vacation hot spot destined to become a retirement locale as well.

Figuring out how close is close enough can be tricky, says Sandra Stern, director of multiple residence and farm advisory group for Citigroup Private Bank. Clients of hers decided on a whim to buy a house on Fire Island that was only 60 miles from their primary home in New York. "They were staying on the island with friends and were cycling down the beach and saw the house on the water," she says. "They fell in love immediately. It was a wonderful turn-of-the-century beach house, and they made an offer on an impulse." Unfortunately, the couple quickly found out that although the house wasn't far away, the 90-minute drive plus 60-minute ferry ride required to get there were serious drawbacks. "Their family didn't want to come out there; even their dog hated the trip," Stern says. The two lucked out when their offer was declined.

Of course, some vacation home buyers opt for locales that are a little more out of the way. Western states are attracting healthy soon-to-be-retirees who want to continue active sports like skiing and hiking that they've enjoyed for a lifetime. "A number of people are moving into low-population western states—Montana, Idaho, Utah, Nevada, and Colorado," says Longino, the Wake Forest University professor and demographer. "In coming years, boomers will seem to flood into these places."

The trick to successful distance vacationing is choosing a place you love. John and Corry Cochol are both educators in Canandaigua, New York. He's a principal of a special education school and she teaches first grade. They have three daughters, aged 22, 20, and 16. For seven years, the family vacationed on the Outer Banks along North Carolina's coast, hundreds of miles from the family's upstate New York home. John had first wanted to visit as a high school student in the Bronx, when he daydreamed of surfing. Traveling south to the warm, windswept beaches was a dream come true for him. Pretty soon, the two started organizing trips for their neighbors and friends. One summer they rented 15 houses from their favorite rental agent. After a while, the two decided that spending only one week a year at the Outer Banks wasn't enough, and they started coming down for three weeks. They got to know the locals, and established friendships that lasted vacation after vacation.

Each year, as the family made their way south, John would ask Corry if she wanted to buy a house in one of the tiny towns studding Hatteras Island. But Corry, who describes herself as the "practical one," said she felt such a move was far too expensive for them. Then, one summer when the family struggled to find a decent house to rent for the following year, Corry remembers the leasing agent turning to her and saying, "Look, you guys are down here so much, you might as well buy a place." For the first time Corry didn't resist, and after scouring the agent's analysis of the taxes and area rentals, she became convinced that they could take on the obligation of a second home.

That week, the pair independently saw a lot for sale that would be perfect for their new home. John saw the lot on his usual morning beach run, and Corry, who likes to walk, spotted it the same day. Plenty of people would have been cautious about building a house long distance, but the couple eagerly snapped up the lot and made plans for construction, visiting twice during the construction to check up on progress. Now they rent out their home 22 to 27 weeks a year and vacation there for three.

Why were they so confident they could pull off owning and running a home long distance? "We've developed a real relationship with the people who work for the realty," she says. "They know my daughter—she goes to school in Salisbury. They watch out for her. One of the reasons we have been so successful is that we know them personally."

Citigroup's Stern says the obvious dedication that a couple like the Cochols have for their vacation home neighborhood is critical to finding the right fit when looking for a second home. "Buying property is like buying art," she says. "You must be passionate about it. You have to be emotionally attached to the property. You're buying it to enjoy your leisure time. There has to be some type of emotional joy that you feel, not only with the rush of the purchase."

Getting a Mortgage

Low interest rates are making second home ownership more affordable than ever for many people. With rates hitting the low 6 percent mark in late 2002, the monthly mortgage on a $162,000 home (the median vacation home price) was only $801 provided you put down 20 percent. Rates this low make a 15-year mortgage look much more affordable as well. Consider, at current rates, a borrower paying a half point down will have to cough up just $1,080 in monthly mortgage payments. (A point equals 1 percent of a mortgage loan. Some lenders charge points to originate a loan.) Think about it: If you're 10 years from retirement, you could have your second home just about paid off by the time you break out your golf clubs. (See Worksheet 8.1.)

Strapped for cash? There's more good news: You may not have to come up with a full 20 percent down payment on your second home. Over the past few years, in a drive to reach more potential customers, more and more lenders are allowing borrowers to put only 10 percent—even less in some cases—down on a second home. Wells Fargo Home Mortgage on the island of Kauai in Hawaii will let you get away with as little as 5 percent down, says Doug Henderson, the branch manager. But he adds that buyers usually want to put down more. "Most second home buyers want to put down 20 percent because they want to keep their mortgage down," he says. (It's not just lenders in exotic locales that are offering low rates. Lender Countrywide Home Loans at www.countrywide.com makes 5 percent down loans on second homes as well.)

As with any mortgage, lenders will pay particular attention to your record of paying down debt. If you have good credit, the increasing use of computerized systems that assign you a credit score may make it easier to get a bigger mortgage, even if you carry a lot of debt.

Can You Buy a Second Home?

Step One
Your Maximum Monthly Payment
To start, figure out how much financing the
bank will provide you with.

1. Gross monthly income $_____

2. Monthly real estate payments (total payment on your first home,
   including principal, interest, taxes, and homeowner's insurance) $_____

3. Monthly installment payments (other real estate, car loans, etc.) $_____

4. Estimated monthly rental income on second home times 0.75* $_____

5. Estimated monthly real estate tax and homeowner's insurance
   on second home $_____

6. Add lines 1 and 4, then multiply by 0.28 $_____

7. Subtract lines 2 and 5 from line 6 $_____

*This is how much you can afford to pay per month under the
"housing ratio."*

8. Add lines 1 and 4, then multiply by 0.36 $_____

9. Subtract lines 2, 3, and 5 from line 8 $_____

*This is how much you can afford to pay per month under the
"total obligation ratio."*
    Compare lines 7 and 9. The lesser amount is the approximate
monthly mortgage payment for which you can qualify. To see
how big a loan you can get with that payment, use the table in
Worksheet 5.2.

---

*Most banks will take into account only 75 percent of your rental income
when determining how much you can borrow. Also, you should know that
most lenders will consider rental income *only* if you've applied for an
investment property loan. Mortgages for investment properties carry
higher interest rates and fees.

(Continued)

WORKSHEET 8.1   Can You Buy a Second Home?

Step Two
Tallying Your Hidden Costs

The costs of owning a second home don't end with the mortgage. Factor these costs into your monthly budget, and adjust.

1. Cost of round-trip travel to your second home	$_____
2. Number of trips you expect to make per month	$_____
3. Multiply line 1 by line 2	$_____
4. Monthly cost of a caretaker (including cleaning and maintenance)	$_____
5. Monthly cost of a security system	$_____
6. Other items (pool cleaning, club dues, gardener, etc.)	$_____
7. Add lines 3 through 6	$_____
8. Subtract line 7 from your mortgage payment in Step One	$_____

To see how big a loan you can carry comfortably with that payment, check the table in Worksheet 5.2.

Step Three
How Much House Can You Buy?

Naturally, the bigger the down payment you have stashed away, the more house you can afford to buy. If you can't come up with 20 percent, many lenders will take much less. But if you're calling the house an investment property, expect to cough up at least 10 percent.

1. Enter the loan amount you can afford	$_____
2. Down payment	$_____
3. Add lines 1 and 2	$_____
4. Closing costs*	$_____
5. Subtract line 4 from line 3	$_____

Line 5 ought to be how much of a second home you can afford now.

---

*Closing costs can vary. If you don't know the typical closing costs in your region, use 3 percent as an estimate.

WORKSHEET 8.1   *(Continued)*

Two things drive your credit score: your past bill-paying record and how extended you are on your available credit. If you have problems with either of these, by all means take steps to make your credit report look better. Find out how by reading "How a Lender Looks at Your Application" in Chapter 5.

What else will lenders consider? Your "housing ratio" and "total obligation ratio." The housing ratio compares your gross monthly income with the amount you need to cover housing expenses, including the mortgage payments on both your primary residence and your second home, while the obligation ratio also includes other debts such as credit-card balances and car loans. Typically lenders don't like to see a housing ratio above 28 percent, but the bigger down payment and the better your credit record and finances, the more flexible your loan officer is likely to be.

Keith Gumbinger, vice president of the mortgage rate data web site, www.hsh.com, says that second home mortgages are becoming more and more like the loans for your primary home. "It's not very different anymore. Usually, you'll have to have a slightly higher down payment [for a second residence], and fees will be slightly higher for inspections, background credit checks, or appraisals."

Unfortunately, banks can't be quite as flexible if you're planning to rent the place out. Indeed, because of the guidelines that underwriters set for mortgage lenders, most don't take rental income into consideration when deciding whether to approve your application. If you need your lender to count that income, you'll have to declare the home as an investment property, which usually means you'll have to pay a higher rate. Wells Fargo's Henderson says that he charges an interest rate three-eighths of a point to a half point higher on second home mortgages where the buyer puts down 20 percent and plans to rent the house out. Not only do customers face a higher interest rate, but they also have to put down more on investment property. Wells Fargo requires a minimum of 10 percent.

If you plan to apply for an investment property mortgage, first find out how much of a property's rental income a lender is willing to consider. Doug Perry, first vice president at Countrywide, says that he typically considers 75 percent of income that could be derived from renting it out. "We assume it's going to be empty 25 percent of the time," he says. Generally, you'll need to document your anticipated rents by showing current leases. If those aren't available, consider showing rental information on comparable homes in your neighborhood.

Another option—particularly for people whose primary homes have swelled in value—is to take out a home equity loan or use the proceeds of a cash-out refinance to float the down payment. Just keep in mind that the IRS considers buying a second home a "personal expenditure," which means you can deduct interest only on the first $100,000 of a home equity loan. Otherwise, if you buy the second home with an ordinary mortgage, you can fully deduct the interest on both of your homes, up to $1 million of combined mortgage debt.

One of the most popular ways of swinging a second home, particularly for individuals who've invested in real estate before, is the 1031 exchange (named after the section of the IRS code that governs taxes on real estate sales). It works like this: Let's say you are willing to sell a property in order to buy your vacation dream house. What you can do is hand over the house you want to sell to a qualified intermediary, who sells it for you and buys the new one. (Banks will often act as intermediaries.) As long as you buy a property of equal or greater value that is in the same category (investors must keep buying investment properties, for example), then you can defer capital gains taxes—until you sell the new property. Or you can simply continue trading up.

Joel Korelitz used the 1031 exchange to switch four single-family homes in Fresno for a resort home in Palm Desert, California. Korelitz got involved in real estate investing back in 1980 as he began to realize that most of his investments were heavily weighted in the technology companies he worked for. About 10 years ago, at the urging of a neighbor, he invested in four modest Fresno homes that he rented out. The homes were worth $120,000 each. Over the years, Korelitz built up $300,000 in equity in the properties. The trouble was that prices in Fresno, which had never been as robust a market as northern California, began to soften. So Korelitz, eager to add to his real estate holdings, which included his primary home in Saratoga and a vacation home at Lake Tahoe, decided to trade up. He had an intermediary buy the properties and put down his $300,000 on a new home in the desert. Now, because the Fresno properties were investments, he'll have to rent out the desert home for a few years so he can meet the IRS requirements for staying in the same category. Still, the investor is more than happy with the result.

"I won't have to pay the tax on the houses until I sell them—I can just keep trading them," says Korelitz.

Taking Care of the Property

For most of us, managing a vacation property is more than a little daunting. Let's face it, finding and vetting renters, securing deposits, keeping the place clean, and making sure the pool is in good condition would require most of us to quit our day jobs. The solution: Hiring a property management company. Most resort communities have property management companies that act as not only rental agents but also caretakers, sort of surrogate landlords for the homeowners. What's more, a good property management company will know details about the local scene that you might unwittingly overlook. Is there a local lodging tax? What are the rules about on-street parking? Is there a limit to the number of people who will be able to rent your home at one time?

When choosing a property management company, there are a number of considerations. You'll want to check refererences and make sure that the agency has a history of managing properties similar to yours. Michael Sarka, executive director of the Vacation Rental Managers Association, suggests going to the rental manager's office to check out how you're greeted before you introduce yourself as a possible source of earnings. The reason? Property managers are becoming more and more involved with renters, providing additional services beyond just sheets and towels. "Renters are less comfortable picking up the key under the third rock," says Sarka. "They want to go to an office and get some information on the area, and pick up their tickets to theater or whatever. They want to be treated as a guest." A property manager can also be useful in helping first-time homeowners figure out how best to prepare their home for renters. One clue: Move the Hummel figurine collection to the closet. Another: Think about offering Internet access via a cable modem or digital subscriber line.

The biggest thing you'll want to understand from any property manager is how much the service will cost. Property management is not an inexpensive service (are you prepared to answer the 800 number at midnight?), and most homeowners will face paying a percentage of the lease value when a tenant is found as well as a percentage of the monthly rent for managing the rental property. In Palm Desert, where Korelitz is renting out his home, Fred Sands Realty charges 10 percent of the rent on an annual basis to find tenants plus 10 percent monthly to manage the property. Holly Jessop, who runs the rental division, says that the charge for tenants can be higher if tenants stay for short terms. But charges can vary dramatically. Kathy Stratton, who sells and manages resort properties for Trupp-Hodnett on St. Simons off the coast of Georgia, says fees can range from 25 to 50 percent when stays are extremely short and managers provide extras like maid service. In Taos, New Mexico, RE/MAX agent Phil Valaika charges 6 percent for getting the tenants and 6 percent for management. "Every community is different," he says.

Some property managers like to pad your bill with lots of hidden fees. Just say no to these kinds of things: charging you to call a repairman, charging you to make copies of bills, or even sticking you with another commission if your tenant renews the lease.

The most nerve-racking side of renting your future retirement home is making sure responsible people occupy the place. Although the Cochols had a great relationship with their management company on Hatteras Island, one early spring week their home was occupied by some nasty people who trashed the house. "The damage was above and beyond what the security deposit would cover," recalls Corry. "The carpets were filthy; mattress covers were torn. Pots and pans were gone or burned. Dishes were broken. I was devastated." Fortunately, the management company cleaned the mess up, replaced broken items, and paid for it themselves. "They were excellent," she says.

Ask any potential property managers how they vet prospective tenants. At a minimum, a manager should do a full credit and employment check. Some managers will go further, for example, contacting previous landlords to find out just how the tenant treats rental property. Finally, be sure your property manager spells out precisely what services you are getting. Some managers take the time to drive by every property they handle each month. Most will arrange bill paying for the home's utilities as well as monitor any security systems. In some resort communities, property managers act like the front desk at a hotel, providing 24-hour check-in for owners' tenants. Others arrange for housekeeping, landscaping, and pool maintenance. However, it'll cost you more—at least 25 percent of the monthly rent.

Tax Time

Our capital gains laws, long the bane of retirees living on investment income, have turned into a real boon, especially where real estate is concerned. Now, thanks to rule changes that went into effect in 1997, married couples can avoid paying any tax at all on up to $500,000 in profit when they sell their home. That's way better than the old rules, which only allowed couples to exclude a maximum of $125,000 from capital gains taxes.

Imagine that you sell your Cleveland home, earning a handsome $150,000 in profit. The law saves you capital gains taxes of 20 percent, or $30,000. An added bonus: If you need to sell the fancy Miami condo, you can get the same exclusion as long as you've made it your primary residence for two years or more. (Under the old rules, you would have used up your one-time capital gains exclusion when you sold the Cleveland house.)

Before you start getting a warm and fuzzy feeling for the IRS, we'll introduce you to the devishly complex rules for renting out your new vacation home. For a user-friendly approach to this topic, we consulted Bill Bischoff, an accountant and longtime SmartMoney.com contributor.

How much tax you owe, he says, depends on just how much time you rent out your abode. There are essentially three different kinds of vacation home landlords for tax purposes: those who rent out rarely, those who rent out a great deal and also use the property themselves a great deal, and those who mostly rent the property out.

The tax implications are easiest to understand if you rarely rent out your house. As long as you don't rent out your home for more than 14 days a year, the IRS doesn't really care. That's right: If the Olympics come to your hometown and you rent your house out to a camera crew, you don't have to report a penny of this income. The IRS considers the home a personal residence. So, simply deduct the interest and property taxes on your Schedule A just as you would for your primary residence.

Okay, that was the easy part. On to the really complex stuff. Once you start renting out your home for more than a couple of weeks a year, the IRS is going to look very differently at what you're doing. If you rent out more than 14 days a year but use the home personally more than 14 days a year or 10 percent of the rental days, whichever is greater, your second home will still be considered a personal residence. (By using it personally, the IRS means any use by friends, family, or anyone else who pays less than the market rental rate.)

Qualifying as a personal residence has its advantages. Uncle Sam lets you deduct interest on up to $1 million of mortgage debt on two personal residences (and up to an additional $100,000 on home equity loans). Property taxes are generally deductible, no matter how many homes you own. If you are lucky enough to own more than two homes, you can pick the two with the most mortgage interest each year—usually the main residence and the vacation home with the biggest loan.

Now for the hard part: accounting for rental income and expenses for your dacha. Basically, there is one way to deduct these expenses incurred while you use the house, and another way to deduct expenses incurred while you rent it out. But if done correctly, there is generally no tax liability for the rental income in these cases.

First, allocate interest and property taxes between rental and personal use. For example, say the home is rented out for three months, used by you for two months, and vacant for seven months.

Since vacant time is considered personal use, you allocate three months' worth or 25 percent of the interest and taxes to the rental period and nine months' worth or 75 percent to personal use. Write off the personal portion of the interest and taxes as itemized deductions on Schedule A. (Note that the IRS has disputed this method in the past, but the tax court, the ultimate authority, has ruled it's okay.)

Now here's the truly difficult part. Your goal will be to reduce your rental income to zero in order to rid yourself of any tax liability. First off, reduce the rental income by 25 percent of the interest and taxes (the portion you incurred while renting, in our example). If there's any rental income left, you can deduct a percentage of operating expenses—maintenance, utilities, association fees, insurance, and depreciation—but only to the point where you eliminate that remaining income. (Don't feel badly if you have to go back and reread this paragraph; as I said, it's complex.)

One detail you won't want to ignore: When you calculate operating expenses, you don't count days the house stood empty. In the example, the house was occupied for only five months, so three months' worth, or 60 percent, of the maintenance, utilities, and so on, goes to the rental period, and two months' worth, or 40 percent, to personal use. That 40 percent evaporates as a totally nondeductible item. On your tax return, you will use Schedule E to report 100 percent of the rental income, 25 percent of the interest and taxes, and 60 percent of the operating expenses. If you're like most people, you'll find that the bottom line on Schedule E will be zero because rental income and expenses will be a wash.

When all is said and done, this tortuous process should allow you to fully deduct interest and taxes (part of it on Schedule A, the rest on Schedule E) and usually have enough operating expenses to wipe out your rental income. Any operating expenses you can't deduct can be carried over to future years. Not a bad deal, once you master all the paperwork.

Finally, if you're the sort of vacation home owner who rents it out a lot and uses it very little, your home will still fall under tax rules for rental properties. Specifically, we're talking about cases where you rent more than 14 days a year, and your personal use doesn't exceed 14 days a year or 10 percent of the rental days, whichever is greater. For example, assume you rent 210 days and vacation 21 days; you have a rental property on your hands. (Vacation for 22 days and you are back under the personal-residence rules.) Interest, property taxes, and operating expenses should be allocated based on the total number of days the house was used. The total number of days used in this example is 231, so the split would be 21/231 for personal use, and 210/231 for rental.

Here, if the money you get from renting the house does not cover the cost of renting it, you can post a taxable loss on Schedule E. But don't start tallying up your deductions just yet. First you must successfully clear the hurdles set up by the IRS—the dreaded passive-loss rules. In general, you can deduct passive losses in a given tax year only to the extent of passive income from other sources (such as rental properties that don't produce gains).

There is an exception. The IRS will let you write off up to $25,000 of passive-rental real estate losses if you "actively participate" and have adjusted gross income under $100,000. Making the day-to-day property management decisions will get you over the active participation hurdle. Unfortunately, the exception is phased out for people with adjusted gross incomes between $100,000 and $150,000, and the IRS says that the exception does not apply anyway when the average rental period is seven days or less. But it's not a total loss: The IRS will let you carry over the passive losses you can't take this year into future years. The reality is that many owners find their hoped-for tax losses deferred by the passive rules.

One more problem: The interest incurred during your personal use (21/231 in our example) is nondeductible, because these homes don't qualify as personal residences. (The personal use portion of property taxes is still deductible on Schedule A.) This means you may actually benefit from slipping in some extra vacation days this year. Then you fall into the previous category we described—which means you can deduct the interest and taxes and usually wipe out your rental income with deductible operating expenses.

Bottom line? Vacation home tax rules are hideously complicated, but they tend to favor owners who rent and use their property in pretty much equal proportions. While the rules generally allow you to wipe out rental income, don't look to your summer cottage massive tax break beyond that. The good news? The complexity of the tax rules certainly hasn't kept people from buying their dream vacation homes. "Every time we drive past the National Seashore sign, and I see the dunes—it's beautiful," exults Corry Cochol about approaching her vacation home along the Outer Banks in North Carolina. "I can't wait to retire there."

9

SELLING YOUR INVESTMENT

Each and every year, more than five million people put their homes on the market and successfully sell their investments. Some do it on their own; others hire a listing agent to market and sell their abodes. If you've religiously followed the steps in this book— carefully managing your home to produce its highest ultimate value— you may be more than a little interested in how much money you can make on your nest; heck, you may even be eager to cash it in. But for most of us, selling a home is an anxiety-producing experience. After all, this is our *biggest single investment.* There's no reason, though, that with a careful plan to ready your home for sale and market it that the experience can't be downright rewarding.

That's what this chapter is all about. We'll start by showing you a couple of important steps you'll want to take before you put your investment on the auction block. You'll learn about the handful of inexpensive and easy improvements that are guaranteed to boost the resale value of your home. Then, we'll walk you through the important steps of hiring an agent, or even going it alone—if you've decided you're game for acting as your own agent. We'll explore the tax implications of selling your abode and even show you an alternative to selling for seniors. Want a fast way to unload a property? Check out Sidebar 9.1 on real estate auctions.

First, Research

Before you even think of calling up a real estate agent, you're going to want to take a reality check. Most people live in their homes seven years before selling. That means prices have changed dramatically while you've been going on with your life, buying braces for the kids and climbing the corporate ladder. What's more, buyers' expectations have been changing (and no doubt rising) at the same time. In other words, you may be completely out of touch with the market.

To get a sense of the competition your house will face, go to Realtor.com, the nation's biggest real estate web site, and check out properties for sale in your town that go for the price you expect to be asking. Are there many homes you'll be competing with? (Fewer are definitely better.) How do the homes compare with yours for square footage? Number of baths? What about extras like decks, fireplaces, and swimming pools? Next, take a look around your own neighborhood. Are you the only one who hasn't upgraded? Is your house the only one with a carport, while everyone else has a finished garage? Does your two-bedroom bungalow have just one bathroom while everyone else's has one and a half or two? If you find a big gap between the amenities of your home and those of your neighbors' home, your expectations for the selling price may be way out of line.

Just one other thing: Make sure you're ready to sell. For people who own a home as an investment, it's a no-brainer decision. You may need the money for your children's education or you may simply be tired of handling multiple properties. But if you're selling the house you live in, you need to make sure you and your spouse are ready for the change. The last thing you want to do is start the ball rolling to sell your abode and then stop midprocess as the two of you become wistful over selling the house where Johnny took his first steps. "It's an emotional transaction," says Ed Mitchell, manager of the Prudential

Speed Selling/Auctions

Thinking about selling your home? You could hire a real estate agent, set some For Sale signs in your front yard, endure endless parades of house hunters traipsing through your living room, and hope and pray that your house sells quickly. However, if you're like most people, selling your house will probably take as much as three months.

But if you're the impatient type, you could do what William and Anne Visser did. They put their house on the auction block.

Their home—a ranch, really—sat on 1,500 acres in northern California. Deer grazed in the meadows surrounding their house, and trout fed in the streams crisscrossing their sprawling property. The home itself was elaborate, with five bedrooms and a library. Redwood beams spanned the ceiling of the great room. One wall was completely glass, so visitors could take in the dramatic views of nearby Mount Shasta. The couple probably would have remained there forever had William's doctor not ordered the gentleman rancher to slow down to keep from aggravating a heart condition. The two decided in 2000 to sell the estate.

The problem was that the property, which they had bought 10 years earlier for $900,000, was unusual. Since they were out in the country, tacking up a For Sale sign beside their driveway would hardly get the attention they needed, much less ensure a fast turnaround. Instead they jumped on a friend's suggestion to hire an auctioneer to sell the property, employing William Bone, head of National Auction Group, one of the top firms in the country.

Bone placed ads for the property in several regional newspapers. Just days before the auction, he opened the house to tours by prospective bidders, who would put up $100,000 certified checks to participate.

Auction day made Anne Visser so nervous she was reminded of her wedding. "I was excited and sad," she says. They set up a tent outside, serving wine and appetizers to the 100 or so people who attended the event. A band played jazz softly. Despite the serene environment, Anne's jitters persisted. The two had planned an "absolute auction," which meant the house would be sold that day, even if the bids were disappointing.

As it turned out, her worries weren't warranted. The auction itself took just 30 minutes and drew 10 bidders. When it was over the house had sold for $2.5 million, more than double the price the Vissers had paid for it. And the transaction had been accomplished in just two months. "We had an unusual property and needed to find a buyer and sell the property quickly," says Anne Visser. "The auction brought together many interested buyers at one time and sold our property right then and there."

You may think of a property auction as something that happens on the courtroom steps, a real desperation sale that is not likely to attract a property's full value. But plenty of homes are being sold at auction, and not all of them are bankruptcy clearance sales or expensive beauties like the Vissers'. Some $52 billion in real estate was sold at auction in 2000, and more than half of that was residential real estate. And the numbers are growing rapidly. Stephen Martin, a real estate auction analyst at the Gwent Group, an Indiana consulting firm, says that the 2000 sales levels are six times higher than those of 1980. One sign that auctions are catching on: Real estate agents are starting to get in on the act.

If an auction appeals to you, though, you'll want to consider the following tips.

Advice for auction sellers: Selling at auction makes sense if you live in a hot housing market and putting a bunch of buyers in one room is almost certain to lead to a bidding war. You might also consider an auction if your house has unusual features like elaborate grounds or a wealth of special built-ins. Tommy Rowell, chairman of the Auction Marketing Institute, says sellers should hire an auctioneer with credentials. (Check out Auctionmarketing.org for details.) "Make sure the auctioneer you hire has successfully

auctioned properties like yours," he says. "Results speak vol-
umes." And think about setting a reserve price in your auction,
a minimum amount that you'll require before signing the place
over.

Advice for auction buyers: Buyers are best advised to
shop auctions when their local market is slow. That's when
they're more likely to identify homes that have lingered on the
market and whose owners are getting antsy. Another good sign
for buyers: The house is one of several similar homes in a new
development. Empty homes are a liability for builders. Make
sure, though, if you're thinking of bidding for a house, to inspect
it before the auction.

SIDEBAR 9.1

Connecticut Realty office in Middletown. "You're dealing with one of
the most stressful things that can happen to people."

Going Out on Your Own

What if you could add a luscious 6 percent to your sales price? You
can—that is, if you sell your house without a real estate agent. More
and more homeowners are choosing to sell on their own, in part because new online tools make it so easy. Alexandra Avenius, the office
manager of an engineering and design firm just outside Detroit,
Michigan, didn't think twice when she decided to sell her tiny two-
bedroom bungalow in suburban Royal Oak to return to Europe. "I
figured I would try to sell it on my own and I could save the costs,"
she says. "The realtors take six percent, and that is quite a chunk."

Avenius had already proven herself a pretty adventurous homeowner. She had bought the house at a discount, paying just
$72,000—$27,500 less than the original asking price—for the fixer
upper, which had been on the market for eight months. "The roof
was wrecked—it rained in the house," she recalls. What's more, the
windows were original to the house's 1927 construction. Avenius

made a number of upgrades to the 770-square-foot home, spending a total of $16,000 to fix the roof, mend the crumbling chimney, and paint the interior.

When it came time to sell, Avenius figured that the best way to market the house to likely buyers—young singles attracted to Royal Oak's restaurants and shops—would be to put it on the Internet. So she spent $20 to list her house on 4SaleByOwner.com (www.4saleby-owner.com), and wrote a detailed description of the property to accompany the picture. She also put a sign up in her yard. While most experts maintain that selling on your own makes the most sense when you're not facing an imminent move, as Avenius was, she sold her house only two weeks after listing it, to the second person who inquired. Price? She got her list price of $106,000. Her costs? Twenty dollars for the Web listing and $1,700 to the title company that drew up the paperwork. "It's really easy," Avenius says. Her savings? $4,640.

She's not the only one. Gomez Research has estimated that by 2005 the "for sale by owner" market (sometimes called the "fizbo" market) will have grown from its current 20 percent share to over 40 percent. It's no wonder. First off, paring the agent's cut of your gains would seem to be one of the easiest ways to make money in a real estate deal. Listing agents pocketed some $35 billion in commissions in 2001's ebullient market. But the real change fueling the fizbo market is the growing reach and sophistication of online sites that not only list properties, but offer other services as well. Steve Udelson, president of Owners Advantage, which operates the Owners.com web site, says his site offers users a suite of services that start with the Internet listing but also include a toll-free number that appears on the Owners.com For Sale sign in your front yard. Buyers can call the number on their cell phones, then plug in a listing ID number, and hear the features of your house immediately, including number of bedrooms and baths, address, square footage, and asking price. Then, if they are interested, they can opt to leave a message for the owner, asking more questions or scheduling an appointment to see the house.

An even bigger innovation, though, is starting to transform the business. Online fizbo sites are offering discount Multiple Listing Service (MLS) listings. That means individuals can get access to the most powerful marketing tool available to the professionals. At GoneHome (www.gonehome.com), users pay $500 and get the standard MLS listing without being obligated to pay the full 6 percent commission for services, says Myron Mullins, chief executive of GoneHome. In fact, the nearly 100 brokers who are part of GoneHome's network and cover 250 markets agree not to solicit the business of clients using the service. GoneHome is available to sellers in 37 states, mostly in larger cities and towns. "It's the holy grail," says Mullins. "There's no doubt about it." The best part? The listings are picked up by the big real estate listing aggregators, like Realtor.com and Yahoo! Real Estate.

You don't have to be Web savvy to sell your home on your own. Back in 1993 when William Supple and his wife were trying to sell their first home in Burlington, Vermont, it was well before the dawning of the age of the Internet. Yet even then Supple was skeptical about the ability of the typical agent to sell his property. The reason? His condominium looked just the same on the outside as all his neighbors' properties. The only hope Supple and his wife had for getting a decent price was to find a way to show the interior, where the two had put in place loads of upgrades.

His solution? He started *Picket Fence Preview*, a publication for sellers who want to market their property on their own. "A lot of people believe it's more complicated than it is—so they are defeated before they even try," says Supple, *Picket Fence Preview*'s publisher and the author of *How to Sell Your Own Home* (Picket Fence Productions, 1996).

If you decide to sell on your own, Supple advises that it's important to hire an appraiser to help you set your selling price. While most people overestimate the value of their home, there are the occasional few who underestimate just how much their property is worth. An appraiser can help you determine the value in the cold, hard light of day. If you've owned your home for a long time—say, 10 years or more—you'll also want to hire a home inspector to review your property. Ask friends for a good inspector and consult www.ashi.org, the site for the American Society of Home Inspectors. That way you'll know the potential problems before a buyer's inspector tells you about them.

Another professional who bears calling early in the process is your attorney. Since most attorneys charge a flat fee for handling a sale, you might as well call yours early so that you can have him or her review all the paperwork as you go from the listing agreement to writing (yes!) the sales contract.

While selling on your own isn't simple, Supple maintains that "properly priced and advertised, a house can sell itself." Sellers should place yard signs and post online ads with local sites aligned with print publications. Worried that the publications are simply throwaways that are never read? Call a few current advertisers to see what kind of responses they are getting.

In fact, you may be the best possible person to showcase your house. "The current owner knows the most about a property," Supple says. "Potential buyers feel like the house is a home when they meet the owners. They relate to it on an emotional level."

Doing it on your own will require you to be more organized and patient. Probably the most intimidating part of the process for first-time fizbo sellers is the close. Hire a good lawyer to advise you on what to disclose and to make sure your contract is ironclad.

Supple figures that most negotiations stumble on a 5 to 10 percent difference in price—just about the amount that a broker requires for his services. "You don't need him," he says.

Hiring an Agent

If you decide to use a real estate agent, best-case scenario, you'd like to have an experience like Goldie Wright and her husband, Vince Outlaw. The San Diego couple listed their house in the suburb Del Cerro for $329,000 in the summer of 2001 and immediately drew three bids over their asking price. Not bad. They accepted an offer for $337,000, which was more than *twice* what they had originally paid for the house. But it gets even better.

Most sellers in rising markets can never pocket the gains they make on their homes because the new house they buy has similarly appreciated in price. But they can use the gains to trade up. Wright, with the help of her agent, located a five-bedroom house about a mile away that had originally been listed at \$499,900. It was perfect for Wright and Outlaw and their two children, Miles and Madeleine. The owners had already reduced the price by \$15,000 after the house had sat for six weeks and drawn no offers. Sensing opportunity, Wright and Outlaw bid a mere \$465,000, and were accepted. *Ka-ching!* "They did well," says their agent, Teri Hill of Hill & Hill Realty, who has seen the same model home sell for as much as \$650,000.

Not everyone can buy and sell as opportunistically as Wright and Outlaw, but if you're planning to use an agent you'll want to shop carefully for the best one. One key? Finding agents with local savvy. Hill has spent her entire real estate professional life working in Del Cerro, where more than 40 years ago her grandparents started the realty firm she works for.

How do you find a winner? Well, most experts recommend interviewing at least three agents to come up with just the right person. That's certainly a good start. But you should also identify those agents who've sold homes successfully in your neighborhood. This will help you find agents who really know how to sell homes in your area—maybe because they live there or maybe because they simply prefer it. Either way, you're getting a real advocate.

When you interview candidates, you'll also want to ask for a comparable sales study of your area. This is simply a list of homes similar to yours that have sold in the town or city you live in. Check to make sure the homes are similar to yours in size and location. Ask for actual sales prices as well as listing prices. Knowing both will help you figure out how long to expect it to take for your house to sell. If you're selling into a market that is slowing, Mark Zervos, founder of Century 21 Leaders in suburban Cleveland, Ohio, suggests paying particular attention to very recent home sales, even if the homes aren't exactly like yours. The reason? Only the most recent sales will show you new price trends and whether it's taking longer for homes on the market to sell. "You can't just look at houses that sold over the last six months, because maybe in the interim the job market has become less stable or the economy has gone down," he says.

One of the most important things your agent will do is to help you price your house. He or she will use the comparable price data to devise a price. But keep this in mind: Some agents use a high initial price as a way to get business. They will boost the price of your house simply to get your listing, a practice called "buying a listing." Let's face it, if you're interviewing three agents and one of them makes the case that he or she can sell your house for considerably more than the other two, it's just human nature to try to get the highest price. If the gambit works, the agent gets a higher commission as well. (This is where it comes in handy to already have an appraisal on hand.)

"Sometimes new agents will fabricate a higher price, not understanding that it can hurt them in the long run," says Lydia Pisano, regional training director for Watson Realty in Orlando, Florida. "You see them taking sellers $10,000 to $20,000 over what should be asked. People drive by and say, 'that's outrageous.'"

Pisano cites a recent example of an agent who put a slightly inflated price of $269,000 on a home, figuring that the strong market should allow him to get the higher price. Fairly quickly, he got an offer of $255,000, still above what Pisano thought the house was worth. But instead of accepting the offer, the owners opted to wait, because they thought their house was worth the original listing price. Unfortunately, the house didn't draw immediate offers, and a few weeks later they were forced to reduce the price to $264,900. "Now it's a stale listing," she says. "The house is still sitting there. It's a divorce situation. Once it becomes a stale listing, you end up getting less than what you could have gotten. There's a sell-by date on these houses just like on a pint of milk. When they stay on the market a long time, people assume there is something wrong with the house."

Another key issue to thoroughly check out: the marketing plan. Ask each agent you interview just how he or she intends to promote your house. Remember, the broader an audience that sees your home, the better. The single tool that agents rely on most is the local Multiple Listing Service (MLS), an association of real estate brokers who share information on listings and also agree to split commissions between the listing broker and buying broker on homes sold through the service. Agents and brokers pay to be members of the service and obtain access to these listings. Not that long ago, the listings were published in books. Carl DeMusz, president and CEO of the Northern Ohio Regional Multiple Listings Service, says he used to publish two compendiums of listings each year—each as fat as a phone book—for the 7,000 members in his system. But the books were out-of-date nearly as soon as they were published, and in 2001 he began putting the listings up on a web site that agents could easily access in a more timely manner.

Today, electronic listings are picked up by Realtor.com, as well as local agents who want to make sure they have the most complete web sites available. Because the MLS is probably the single most important tool in selling your home, you'll want to make sure your agent picks a photo to put on the Web that shows your home to its best possible advantage. An MLS listing will help your home be seen by the biggest potential group of possible buyers. Some agents will also help you put up sweeping 360-degree views of your house that will show off interiors and landscaping. Ask ahead of time whether your agent is adept enough technically to produce one of these mini-movies. And make sure that the listing goes up on the Web pronto.

The MLS isn't the only game in many towns. Zervos in Cleveland says he buys out the back page of the local newspaper's weekly real estate guide to make sure homes are seen by serious and even casual shoppers. Your agent should be taking similar steps. Skimping on promotion is one way agents can keep more of their commissions.

Check your listing contract for any special fees or assessments. Some agents will charge a cancellation fee of 1 or 2 percent of the asking price if you cancel your listing agreement before the typical 90-day contract expires.

Prepping Your Investment for Sale

Plenty of homeowners preparing their houses for sale panic, worrying that they need to do major upgrades to attract buyers. But in markets where demand is either steady or rising, you won't need a big project to get buyers' attention. "People think they have to upgrade their bathroom with Italian tile," says Brad Inman, founder of Home-Gain.com, a web site that matches home buyers and sellers with agents. "It's not about home improvements. It's about getting the house cleaned up. It's like a date: Put on a nice suit." His advice? Mow the lawn, plant some brightly colored plants at the entrance to the house, and whatever you do, he says, open up the curtains throughout the house so it appears bright and airy.

Beth Pressler, sales director at Higbie Maxon Agney Realtors in Detroit's upscale Grosse Pointe suburb, says she usually walks through the house room by room with the seller, giving advice on how each corner of the house can be spruced up. Her suggestion: Take care of the small things that can easily turn off potential buyers. She advises smokers to have their carpets cleaned and to spritz furniture and drapes with an odor-removing product like Febreze. Then she tells them not to smoke in the house until it's sold. Clean the kitty litter once a day. "Get out the clutter. Rent a storage unit and put your knickknacks and extra furniture away," she says. "Make sure your home can actually be seen by the new buyer." When you get done clearing out the place, the goal is to make the home "look like a model home, but lived in."

If you're selling a home that's an investment property, Bob Cain, publisher of the newsletter *Rental Property Reporter*, suggests giving your tenants the heave-ho. "Tenants are a pain to work around," he says. "Do whatever it takes to get the tenants out; then you have a vacant house and it's easier to show. You don't make appointments, and you can simply use a lockbox [to keep a set of keys in]." He recalls the tenants who didn't want to leave the house they were renting, and told potential buyers there was a roof leak. "It was a crock," Cain recalls.

Here's one other pointer to getting your house ready, whether it's a first or second home: Plain is better. Buyers like to imagine their own furnishings in a home, and no matter how much you like your leopard-patterned wall-to-wall, well, it's not going to sell your house. Debbie Mottl, an agent in the Cleveland, Ohio, suburb of North Royalton, can attest to that fact. When she got the listing for the brick-faced four-bedroom, two-and-a-half-bath home with nine-foot ceilings and Jacuzzied master, she thought she'd hit pay dirt. Surely there couldn't be an easier listing to sell. North Royalton's real estate market wasn't red-hot, but it was brisk enough to land a buyer for this beauty. There was just one nagging little problem. The current owners loved wallpaper, and they mixed wallpapers with different designs in the same room. For example, the dining room alone had three different wallpaper designs— a stripe, a floral, and a border that featured a different floral pattern. The other quirk? The wall coverings were all different shades of blue— throughout the house. All the rooms, with the exception of two of the bedrooms, were given similar treatment.

Mottl first asked the couple gently whether they would consider taking the paper down. "I told them we usually neutralize everything," she recalls. But the answer was a quick no. "They had just put it in a year before. They didn't want to spend the money [to remove it]. Plus, for the wife, it was heartbreaking to have it taken out." She then advised them to lower the price to take into account the cost of having the wallpaper removed, which she figured would be about $2,000. But the couple balked at that suggestion, too. It wasn't until three offers fell apart over the wallpaper that the couple agreed to make changes. Before they had a chance to take it out, though, Mottl got an offer for $15,000 below the asking price, and the couple, wearied by the process, agreed to take it. Mottl couldn't help but think that had they just spent the $2,000 first thing and stripped off the wallpaper, they could have sold quickly—*and* gotten their asking price.

"Buyers don't like decorating surprises," she says. "You have to appeal to nine out of ten buyers."

One way to find out exactly what homebuyers in your neighborhood will expect is to go to HomeGain.com's Home Sale Maximizer tool. HomeGain interviewed 2,000 real estate agents to find out what improvements create value neighborhood by neighborhood. By entering your zip code, you can find out which renovations will give you the biggest bang for the buck, and which are absolute must-haves.

Little Renovations with a Big Impact

If you've scouted the competition on foot and on the Internet, it may have become clear that your house needs a little boost, a competitive edge, to get the attention of buyers. Of course, you could go out and spend a fortune, installing, say, state-of-the-art professional kitchen appliances. But if you're getting ready to move, you may want to save any extra dough to upgrade your new house. That means you'll want to think small. The average homeowner spends only $3,000 on home improvement, according to the American Express Retail Index. That's not much to lay out, especially if your home is being sold in a competitive market. A small improvement can be just the gimmick your home needs when the time it takes to sell homes in your neighborhood is getting longer and longer, a sure sign of a slowing market.

To be sure, you'll want to pick your project shrewdly. Nothing gets buyers' attention more than improvements to kitchens and bathrooms. "That's where you get the most bang for your buck," says Lou Manfredini, radio host and author of "Mr. Fix-It" books. Indeed, according to *Remodeling* magazine's annual Cost vs. Value Report, about 80 percent of what you spend on a kitchen remodel can be automatically added to the total worth of your home. Bathrooms are another excellent bet, delivering an 88 percent return.

But where exactly should you start? We asked Manfredini and other home-improvement experts for some ideas. Our first goal: projects that will provide a profound makeover without requiring you to take out a second mortgage. At the same time, we want improvements that are popular right now with homeowners and real estate agents alike—yet are basic enough that you can handle them yourself. Here are three enhancements that can boost your home's appeal for a song.

NO. 1: THE KITCHEN ISLAND (COST, $700 AND UP)

Anyone who has thrown a party knows that people always congregate in the kitchen. Adding an island is one easy way to turn the room into more of a lounge.

The latest kitchen trend is the scaled-down island, and it's pretty simple to install. For a typical six-foot-long version, all you'll need is some cabinetry, a countertop big enough for a one-foot overhang, a couple of stools—and voilà, you're done. At Home Depot, we found two 30-inch oak-finish cabinets for $350 and a $250 laminate countertop. Start by attaching two-by-fours to the floor to anchor the base. Then you just slide the cabinets on top. You don't even have to rip up your old flooring. (A caveat: You'll need plenty of space—about 70 square feet—to make it work, giving you at least 42 inches of clearance on all sides.)

For the most resale appeal, splurge on a granite countertop. Unlike laminate, which chips and stains more easily, granite is durable and burnproof, and "everyone in the world seems to want it," says Bob Vila, host of the syndicated television series *Home Again*. This will boost your budget, though. Granite can cost $120 to $180 a square foot.

If you don't have enough open space for an island, you can still renovate your kitchen on the cheap. Start by yanking up your old linoleum flooring—a big turnoff to potential homebuyers—and replacing it with ceramic tiling (expect to spend about $300 for a typical 10-by-12 kitchen). Next, get rid of those Gidget-era cabinets. New wood or laminate cabinet doors will set you back only about $120 each. Throw in new hinges, put in some slide-out shelves, and the whole setup will pass for new.

NO. 2: THE BATHROOM OVERHAUL (COST, $500 AND UP)

The bathroom is the modern-day sanctuary, says Deborah Sauls-DeLa Cruz, a New York–based interior designer. "These days people practically live there." If you have at least $25,000 to spare, you can really go to town and create a virtual minispa, complete with double vanity sink, separate closet for the toilet, and steam room.

But you don't have to be that ambitious. That 88 percent return on your investment, according to *Remodeling* magazine, applies to even modest makeovers. Given that Home Depot's starting price for bathroom installations is $5,000—which buys you labor but not actual materials—you may want to take on this project yourself. "If you give yourself a $500 budget and do the work yourself, you can get pretty far," says Vila. "Buy some mirrors, lighting fixtures, maybe some one-foot-square mirrored tiles, and it's a very affordable way to accomplish a change of feeling."

We started with the tub, which for about $30 you can make look almost new with a fresh layer of glaze: Simply coat on epoxy, which is basically a sticky paint. Epox is a gold-standard brand; you'll need about one quart, and an open window: This stuff smells strong, which explains why many homeowners are happy to pay about $300 for a contractor to do the job.

Then, redo the floors and walls in ceramic tile for roughly $350 (assuming about a 5-by-7 space). New features are an easy fix, too: Pedestal sinks tend to attract prospective buyers most, says Sauls-DeLa Cruz, and start at roughly $400. And your old toilet? The trend is elongated bowls (starting at about $150, for a traditional model like American Standard).

For about twice that you can also get a motor-equipped "power flush" model—the $360 Toto UltraMax, for example—that uses the same amount of water as your old model but flushes more efficiently.

Again, don't be afraid to think small. When Sheri Loose, an advertising sales representative in Dallas, decided to revamp her bathroom last May, replacing her wobbly toilet was a big priority. But after reading the tips on CornerHardware.com, a do-it-yourself retail and information web site, she found that rather than replacing the whole thing, she could just take the plastic covering off the toilet base and tighten the two main bolts with a wrench. It took all of 15 minutes and didn't cost her a penny. For the rest of the room, the 36-year-old divorced mother painted the walls, replaced a light fixture, and set up new towel bars, all for less than $200 out-of-pocket. "It's made a huge difference," she says. "The bathroom used to be pretty dreary, and now it's much brighter and looks great."

NO. 3: THE BASEMENT WINE CELLAR (COST, $2,000 AND UP)

Wine cellars have become so popular, says Manfredini, that he has installed them in eight of the last 10 homes he's worked on. And since it involves such a tight space, a wine cellar won't bust your savings account. The best area for a wine cellar is an unused 10-by-10 nook. If you have an older home with a stone foundation, "you probably already have an old room that was once a jelly cupboard" or a basic pantry, says Vila. If you don't have a lot of room to play with, you could even consider transforming a closet (one under a flight of stairs is perfect—it's the right size, and tends to stay dry).

For a wine cellar, stone walls are ideal: They look stylish and keep the temperature down in summer (55 degrees is optimum). If your basement walls aren't stone, consider wrapping the room in quarter-inch-thick oak or cedar, both of which absorb moisture and protect the wine. An oak wall—the aesthetic favorite—will cost about $1,200, says Sauls-DeLa Cruz. If you're a purist, add a small chilling unit that keeps both temperature and humidity down. (Manfredini recommends the WhisperKool models, $999 at www.klwines.com.) Then add wine racks, which you can buy in stackable units or have custom-built (and easily spend thousands of dollars). Two quick-fix solutions: At WineAccents.com, we found stackable pine racks that hold 12 bottles each (three for $51), and at Wine.com, we saw a 36-bottle one-piece unit for $86.

The only downside? Unless you sell to an enthusiastic wine lover, putting in a cellar isn't a blue-chip addition. "It's a popular project," Manfredini says, "but it's not a dollar-for-dollar thing. I'd be surprised if you recouped 40 percent of your costs." But it will make your home stand out from the crowd.

Setting the Right Offering Price

Here's a seller's worst nightmare: You carefully groom your home and prepare it for sale. But when you hold your first open house . . . nothing happens. That was pretty much the experience that Ed Mitchell, now manager of the Prudential Connecticut Realty office in Middletown, had when he marketed a three-bedroom colonial in nearby Torrington. He performed a market analysis, and recommended that the sellers list at $124,000. The owners thought $132,000 was a fairer price, and Mitchell listed it for the higher price tag. What happened? Not a thing. Nobody called to see the house. When Mitchell catered a lunch for brokers to tour the property, he found himself alone; after a while, he invited the next-door neighbor over to share lunch—"I was so lonely," he recalls. After the house had been on the market for months, the owners finally agreed to cut the price to the level he originally suggested, and within five days a buyer came along and snapped up the property.

Price is the most important consideration when you list your property. Carl DeMusz, president and CEO of the Northern Ohio Regional Multiple Listings Service, sees more homes moving on and off the market than even the busiest real estate agent observes. Active listings on the MLS he runs for northern Ohio totaled about 23,723 homes through the first eight months of 2002. So when DeMusz talks about why homes don't move, he's worth listening to. His top three reasons homes languish: The home is priced wrong, it's got maintenance issues, or it's functionally obsolete (four bedrooms, one bath). And here's the kicker: The only way to get the house sold regardless of which of these three problems your suffering from? Lower the price. "Everything comes down to price," he says.

If you're putting the house on the market at a time that prices are rising and the time it takes to sell a property is getting shorter, some agents recommend pricing your house a little below market. That's exactly what sellers in San Francisco's popular Noe Valley did at the height of the dot-com rush. What happened next? You guessed it— just like the seller ordered—a bidding war would typically erupt, resulting in stratospheric prices.

If your market is getting weaker rather than stronger, pricing a house below market is a recipe for disaster. This is no time to play games; set your listing price right in line with recent sales of similar properties. Of course, what many homeowners do when prices are falling is simply hold their houses off the market to wait for better conditions.

One other step you might consider, if the market is weak and you absolutely have to sell your home, is to offer seller financing to potential buyers. In this case, you collect a down payment up front from the buyer, say 3 to 5 percent of the purchase price of the house. Then you set up monthly mortgage payments due from the buyer that are slightly higher than the payments on a conventional mortgage (because, after all, you are taking on the risk that a bank normally would). Few buyers will walk away from their down payment.

Alternatives to Selling for Seniors

If you're over 62 and own your home free and clear, one way to cash out your house without selling it is with a reverse mortgage. It works like a running tab, liquidating the equity in your home as you take out cash and accrue interest charges. You can opt to receive the money as a lump sum, an indefinite number of monthly install-ments, or a credit line (usually the best option), and no repayment is due until you die or sell the house. The older you are, the more you can borrow. You can calculate just how much at the AARP's web site (www.aarp.org/revmort).

In the late 1980s reverse mortgages got a bad rap because borrow-ers sometimes were required to pay them back on a set date. The worst-case scenario could mean forcing an elderly couple from their home to repay the lender. Later versions of reverse mortgages were onerous in a different way: Homeowners had to split any appreciation with the lender. Today few reverse mortgages have a set term, and price gains typically go to the homeowner. Any loss is eaten by the lender's insurer.

Because reverse mortgages carry this added risk for the lender, you can expect to pay more in interest and fees, which are deducted from your equity rather than paid out-of-pocket. Interest rates are variable, tied to the one-year Treasury bill plus a margin of 1.5 to 2.1 percentage points. Because of significant up-front costs (totaling 4 percent of your home's value) and monthly servicing fees ($25 to $35), a reverse mortgage makes financial sense only if you plan to stay in your house for a while—at least six to eight years. Otherwise, you'll come out ahead selling your home outright or taking out a home-equity line of credit.

But while that credit line may turn out to be cheaper, it does have the drawback of requiring monthly payments—difficult if the whole reason you're taking the loan is to generate cash flow. Ultimately, the question of whether or not to take a reverse mortgage comes down to this: How much is it worth to you to increase your ability to stay in your home through your golden years?

The Close

Once your hard work has paid off with an offer for your house that is at (or maybe even above) your listing price, you may be tempted to sit back and relax. Our advice? Save the party for later. This is just the beginning of the closing.

First things first. After you've accepted the offer, the buyers will have the property inspected. If you already had the property inspected just before putting it on the market, there should be no surprises. If you didn't, there may be more negotiating ahead. Once the two of you have agreed on any contingencies, Watson Realty's Pisano suggests asking for what she calls a "net sheet," basically just a detailed accounting of the money you expect to walk away with at the closing. This may sound simple—aren't you supposed to simply get a check for the agreed price?—but in reality you'll likely have to subtract fees that will cover the broker's charges, title insurance, documentation stamps, satisfaction of the mortgage (that's the charge it takes to pay off the house and record the deed), plus any prorated taxes.

10

REIT INVESTING

magine it: You're a property baron, a regular Donald Trump. Every month, you collect millions from the tenants in your gold-encased office towers and five-star hotels.

It's a nice fantasy, all right. But the fact is, most of us don't have The Donald's famous touch—not to mention his access to capital. That's why real estate investment trusts make so much sense for many individual investors. They give you entry into big-time real estate without any of the hassles of management. That's right. No 4 A.M. calls from tenants. No detailed record keeping. No refereeing tenant disputes.

Real estate investment trusts (REITs) are, simply put, publicly traded companies that own and manage real estate, whether it's offices, shopping malls, apartments, warehouses, or even mobile home parks. Of the total $4.58 trillion in U.S. real estate market value, REITs own the biggest chunk at 39 percent. (Pension funds rank a close second with 38 percent.) Without REITs, there would be no way for small investors to get a piece of some of the nation's best-known properties, like the Sears Tower in Chicago or the Embarcadero Center in San Francisco or Citigroup's headquarters in New York.

But the real beauty of REITs for individual investors is their unusual structure. Unlike other public companies, REITs must—by law—distribute 90 percent of their taxable income as dividends to shareholders. Yield-hungry investors are taking notice. In 2002, the sector's dividend yield was 7.62 percent. The S&P 500, on the other hand, returned a measly 1.78 percent. To be sure, REITs' total returns—counting appreciation—typically aren't as impressive as conventional stocks. But a bear market for stocks has changed that. Compound annual returns for the group for the 10-year period through October 2002 were 10.05 percent, better than long-term government bonds, which returned 8.19 percent over the period, and even topping the S&P 500, which returned 9.88 percent. (See Figure 10.1.) Although Congress allowed the formation of real estate investment trusts back in 1960, it has only been in the past decade that the industry has matured enough to attract serious investors. In the past few years, REITs' popularity has become even greater as conventional

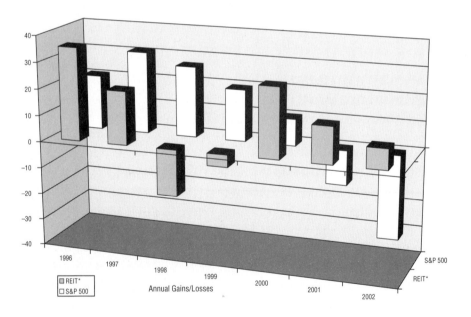

FIGURE 10.1   REIT Performance versus S&P 500
Source: National Association of Real Estate Investment Trusts®.

stocks have underperformed their long-term averages. While stocks generally languished in a bear market, REITs shone. The Morgan Stanley REIT Index rose 27 percent in 2000 and 13 percent in 2001 as the S&P 500 fell 10 percent and 13 percent, respectively.

REITs may continue to have momentum in the next several years for two reasons: First, investors' increasing preference for dividend-paying investments, and second, the fact that the majority of REITs are small-cap and mid-cap stocks, sectors that should perform well as the economy recovers from the recession. While it's not clear whether REITs can continue to outdistance the broader indexes quite so handily as they have in recent years, it is true that adding REITs to a portfolio of more conventional stocks and bonds not only raises returns over the long run, but serves as a counterbalance to other asset classes. According to the research firm Ibbotson Associates, a portfolio comprised half of stocks, 40 percent bonds, and 10 percent Treasury bills would have returned 11.8 percent on average each year between 1972 and 2000, while exposing its owner to 11.2 percent risk. By changing the allocation mix to 40 percent stocks, 20 percent REITs, 30 percent bonds, and 10 percent Treasury bills, the return rises to 12.2 percent while risk drops to 10.8 percent.

Getting Started

The problem you'll encounter, though, if you get serious about REIT investing is figuring out just where to start. There are 177 REIT stocks in the marketplace with $163.49 billion in assets as of mid-2002. One way to start winnowing that large group is to kick out the mortgage REITs, 19 of the total. As their name suggests, mortgage REITs buy and sell mortgages, not properties. Their returns are mostly a function of the manager's ability to predict and trade on changes in interest rates. If you're interested in getting your share of terra firma, you'd do better to shop elsewhere. While you're at it, also knock out the hybrid REITs, which are a mix of mortgage and equity REITs. That should leave you with a universe of just 151 equity REITs.

Next, you'll want to check out the different property sectors: offices, apartments, retail, industrial/warehouse, hotels, and manufactured homes, among others.

Office

The office sector of the REIT industry is by far the largest, accounting for 28 percent of the entire $163.49 billion industry. Experienced REIT investors consider office REITs a core holding because the sector's long leases—suburban office leases span three to five years and downtown leases can run five years or more—serve as a cash cushion, making the business far more predictable than others. Operating margins are a lush 65 to 70 percent. Even when a company breaks a lease early, it pays a hefty fee to get out of the contract. As a result, the industry nationally hasn't had a single quarter when absorption of new space turned negative in the eighteen years between 1982 and 2000, says Jim Bracken, an analyst at the real estate research firm Green Street Advisors. The industry is dominated by three players—Equity Office Properties (ticker symbol: EOP), Boston Properties (BXP), and Trizec Properties (TRZ)—which together account for more than half the sector's market capitalization. (For a bird's-eye view of the office REIT market, see our interview with Sam Zell in Sidebar 10.1.)

However, while the office sector's results are initially resistant to recessions—because of those long leases—bad times eventually do catch up. The economic expansion of the 1990s was great for managers of office properties. The boom hit a fever pitch in 2000 when space demands from the technology bubble drove vacancy rates down to 8.6 percent (see Figure 10.2). But as the tech industry cratered, the dynamics of the office leasing business faltered, exposing the excesses of the boom. "People were stockpiling space—they ordered office space two years ahead of their needs," says Ralph Block, executive vice president and chief REIT portfolio manager at Bay Isle Financial. Tech companies subleased space they could no longer use. By 2002, even the sublease tenants were starting to melt away in the worst of markets. Office rents in San Francisco, which had hit $80 to $90 a

Sam Zell, Q&A

A true contrarian, Sam Zell earned the nickname "Grave Dancer" for famously snapping up distressed real estate in the property bubble burst of the late 1980s. These days, he's better known as the father of publicly traded real estate investment trusts, having founded the nation's largest REIT, Equity Office Properties, back in 1976. (He continues to serve as the company's chairman.) As always, he still is on the lookout for value investing opportunities.

Q: *How do you find value in the real estate market?*

A: My own formula is very simple. It starts and ends with replacement cost because that is the ultimate game. In the late 1980s and early 1990s, I was the only buyer of real estate in America. [People asked me] "How could you buy it?" How could I project yields? Rents? For me, it came down to these issues: Is the building well built? Is it in a good location? How much less than the cost of replacement is its price? I bought stuff for 30 cents on the dollar and 40 cents on the dollar.

Sam Zell

Real estate is all about supply and demand. If I own the supply at a cost of X and the cost of replacement is 2X, then I like my position.

Q: *Do you see much value in the commercial real estate market now?*

A: The issue today is there are no deals out there. There is no one in trouble, no one hanging from the rafters or jumping from the windows in the real estate industry on the commercial side. Despite the fact that markets have softened and vacancies have increased, and cash flows are down, the real story is that leverage is down even more. Nobody ever went broke because their cash flow went from $2 million to $1 million.

Q: *What type of REIT among the many varieties such as office and retail shows the most promise for investors?*

A: Mobile home parks have the most opportunity. It is the greatest business since sliced bread. I took MHC (Manufactured Home Communities) public—the largest in that arena—in February 1993. I went to Wall Street and they said, "Trailer parks—are you kidding?" I explained it to them very simply. Seventy-six percent of our tenants have no mortgage because our business is retiree mobile home parks. I own the land. They come in and place their house on my land. I'm not a subordinated creditor. The key to this deal is I'm always first. My bad debt loss is zero. These people are buying a lifestyle.

Q: *Why have housing prices been so strong for so long?*

A: We've just come through 10 years of what will be looked back on as the greatest monetization event ever. The American public has a lot of money—particularly the upper end—and the question is what do you do with the money—collect 2 percent in the bank or collect irreplaceable assets? The rise in single-family house prices is following the rise in reproduction costs. Single-family houses in the last three years have gone up three times the inflation rate. You have too much money chasing too few opportunities.

Q: *There's been a lot of talk about whether real estate prices have risen too far too fast, and whether we're headed for a crash in prices. What do you think about prices?*

A: It's not a bubble. What you are seeing is the overall price level of single-family housing moving up to a new plateau. Do you ever wonder why the price of housing is three times higher in Germany than it is in the United States? Everywhere else in the world, housing is a much more significant part of your cost of living than it is here. We have the cheapest housing in the world by a big margin.

SIDEBAR 10.1

square foot at the best of times, cratered to $30 a square foot. Nationally, vacancies rose to 16 percent.

To be sure, that kind of down cycle isn't unusual. In fact, the office market is typically cyclical, and savvy investors learn how to play the cycles like a previous generation of semiconducter investors learned the gyrations of companies in the chip business. Jim Costello, senior economist at Torto Wheaton Research, doesn't see recovery on the horizon until the second half of 2003 at the earliest. That current pessimism bodes well for office REITs over the next few years if the economy's recovery proceeds as expected. But the best REIT investors will continue to watch for signals that overbuilding is starting again— the sector's Achilles' heel. Block predicts that rents may come under pressure in many markets in 2005 to 2007 as older, higher-rate leases expire and rents have to readjust to lower lease rates among competitors. The trick to investing in the office sector is finding the companies with stong management teams and solid balance sheets that can weather the occasional storms, and even use downturns to pick up bargain properties.

Apartments

As the name suggests, apartment REITs build, manage, and/or run apartment complexes. The group includes some 19 companies with a

Year	Vacancy Rate (%)	Rent Growth (%)	Construction Rate (%)
80	NA	NA	7.25
81	NA	NA	7.07
82	NA	NA	8.70
83	NA	NA	7.72
84	NA	NA	8.23
85	NA	NA	8.04
86	NA	NA	7.52
87	18.50	NA	5.69
88	18.00	NA	4.40
89	18.00	−2.89	4.51
90	18.60	0.65	3.23
91	19.00	−3.01	1.97
92	18.50	−9.66	1.15
93	16.80	1.58	0.27
94	15.20	6.76	0.21
95	13.80	8.31	0.27
96	12.10	3.84	0.59
97	9.80	11.73	1.02
98	8.90	7.23	1.97
99	9.60	7.28	3.47
00	8.60	14.01	2.83
01	14.20	−6.71	2.78
02	16.20	−9.19	2.23
03	14.50	2.60	1.37
04	12.80	5.73	1.90
05	12.00	5.04	2.09
06	11.80	3.72	2.32
07	11.80	3.52	2.46

FIGURE 10.2 The Outlook for the Office Sector
Source: Torto Wheaton Research, a business unit of CB Richard Ellis.

total market cap of $27.45 billion. The industry is dominated by national operators like Equity Residential (EQR) and Archstone-Smith Trust (ASN), but smaller upstarts, like Los Angeles–based Arden Realty (ARI), focus on specific regions. In recent years, the two groups have been merging as the big players gobble up smaller players to jump-start operations in attractive markets.

Like office REITs, apartment REITs are regarded as a core holding. (See Figure 10.3.) But while it's the predictable nature of office REITs that investors find appealing, apartment REIT buyers in the past often touted the defensive nature of the apartment business as the quality they liked most. When times are bad and companies start laying people off, it's usually the youngest workers who get booted first. As a result, the number of apartment dwellers increases as home ownership becomes a less viable option. History didn't repeat itself in the downturn of 2001. Not only did wages remain fairly steady, but low interest rates encouraged many renters to buy. While a handful of markets like Washington, D.C. and southern California remained strong through the bad times, rents and REITs suffered in the San Francisco Bay area and Atlanta, among other markets.

What may be happening is that the nature of the rental market is changing—and broadening—something that could ultimately be good for apartment REIT owners. While apartments used to be just for young couples starting out, some apartment dwellers don't make the leap to home ownership because they prefer the flexibility of rentals. Some have been priced out of the market. Further, some empty nesters are opting to rent so that they can enjoy city life before retiring.

Meanwhile, the future of the apartment industry's core audience—young singles and couples—looks upbeat. Lehman Brothers REIT analyst David Shulman says that during the decade ending in 2009, population in the key renter group, people aged 20 to 34 years old, is expected to rise 2.8 million and reach 58.5 million, after a long decline over the previous decade of 7.2 million. Only another recession or a slowdown in immigration could threaten those trends, he says.

Apartment REITs have struggled in the past couple of years as the single-family home market has taken off, but a broad-based recovery

Year	Vacancy Rate (%)	Rent Growth (%)	Construction Rate (%)
80	5.98	9.06	1.80
81	6.23	8.58	1.56
82	6.70	7.31	1.77
83	7.00	5.71	2.81
84	7.93	5.30	3.05
85	9.15	6.14	3.15
86	9.70	5.68	2.87
87	9.85	4.11	2.02
88	9.25	3.80	1.76
89	8.98	3.88	1.47
90	9.40	4.26	1.08
91	9.38	3.48	0.58
92	9.43	2.43	0.50
93	9.03	2.29	0.58
94	9.00	2.49	0.87
95	9.23	2.43	1.00
96	8.95	2.67	1.07
97	9.00	2.96	1.18
98	8.70	3.28	1.34
99	8.63	3.11	1.34
00	8.85	3.70	1.29
01	8.80	4.53	1.27
02	9.65	3.78	1.32
03	NA	2.73	1.13
04	NA	2.61	1.01
05	NA	2.68	0.93
06	NA	2.90	0.90
07	NA	3.11	0.91

FIGURE 10.3 The Outlook for the Apartment Sector
Source: Torto Wheaton Research, a business unit of CB Richard Ellis.

should be a spur for these stocks. Not only would it drive more consumers to rent apartments for themselves as incomes rise, but it would also boost inflation, a trigger that would set in motion rent increases. The profitability of the apartment market, like the office market, is sensitive to overbuilding. What's more, investors in the sector's smaller stocks will want to pay particular attention to the markets where they do business since the health of the economy can vary greatly state to state and even city to city.

Retail

Talk about contrarian. While the rest of the stock market (and many REIT sectors) tanked in 2002, the retail sector was on fire. (See Figure 10.4.) Total returns rose 14.5 percent through October 2002 as consumers continued to spend regardless of the anemic broader economy.

But the strong performance masks a complex sector in which returns can vary by type of development. There are regional malls, superregional malls, strip centers, and power centers. The easiest way to keep them straight is to think in terms of the consumer to whom they appeal. Start with the higher-end shopper who frequents full-fledged regional shopping malls and superregional malls with one million square feet of retail space or more. Department stores and specialty retailers do business in these settings. Rents and sales per square foot here are the highest in the business. But so are costs. Mall REITs weren't even available until 1992, when several mall developers began taking their companies public, such as Herbert and Melvin Simon and Alfred Taubman. The largest today in the $17.67 billion business is Simon Property Group (SPG), with a market cap of $6.31 billion.

If malls were one of the developments of choice of the last boom in real estate, power centers are the next. Smaller and more accessible, power centers offer shoppers far fewer options but give them convenience and access. They can range in size from 200,000 square feet to 700,000 square feet. The centers are dominated by the retail stars of the 1990s—Wal-Mart, Target, Home Depot, and Kohl's. Big players

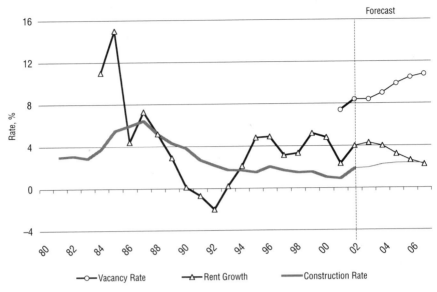

Year	Vacancy Rate (%)	Rent Growth (%)	Construction Rate (%)
80	NA	NA	NA
81	NA	NA	3.00
82	NA	NA	3.09
83	NA	NA	2.87
84	NA	11.00	3.75
85	NA	15.00	5.50
86	NA	4.40	5.96
87	NA	7.30	6.44
88	NA	5.20	5.19
89	NA	2.90	4.31
90	NA	0.10	3.83
91	NA	−0.70	2.70
92	NA	−2.00	2.18
93	NA	0.20	1.73
94	NA	2.10	1.69
95	NA	4.80	1.51
96	NA	4.90	2.04
97	NA	3.10	1.68
98	NA	3.30	1.46
99	NA	5.20	1.53
00	NA	4.80	1.02
01	7.40	2.30	0.89
02	8.40	4.00	1.84
03	8.40	4.30	1.92
04	9.00	4.00	2.21
05	9.90	3.20	2.34
06	10.50	2.60	2.36
07	10.80	2.20	2.29

FIGURE 10.4 The Outlook for the Retail Sector
Source: Torto Wheaton Research, a business unit of CB Richard Ellis.

in this category include Developers Diversified Realty (DDR) and Kimco Realty (KIM).

The draws for neighborhood centers are grocery stores, drugstores, and the kinds of small-scale businesses like restaurants and package delivery services that never go out of style. If any sector can claim recession resistance, this is the one. Groceries and drugstores, the key tenants, sometimes called anchor tenants, are so pivotal to the success of these developments that their rent is often computed as a percentage of sales. Neighborhood centers are typically 80,000 to 150,000 square feet in size. Torto Wheaton's Costello says that the economics of operating these stores improved during the 1990s as margins on existing goods and the kinds of goods have widened, improving fortunes for the neighborhood centers where they do business. That success is beginning to draw new competition as Wal-Mart, the big-format mass merchant, rolls out smaller-scale grocery/drugstores. Neighborhood center REIT operators include Weingarten Realty (WRI) and Pan Pacific Retail Properties (PNP).

The new retail trend is a blending of all these types into "lifestyle centers" that include entertainment, mall merchants, and restaurants. In a typical lifestyle center, shoppers might drop into the Pottery Barn, eat lunch at Panera Bread, and then catch a movie, says Merrill Lynch analyst Craig Schmidt. Federal Realty (FRT) is the big player in this small but growing retail sector.

Industrial/Warehouse

These are the buildings you probably rarely see—distribution centers, bulk warehousing facilities, and light manufacturing space that more and more often are found in a ring around airports. Industrial and warehouse REITs represent just 6 percent of the industry, with $10.2 billion in market capitalization.

The industrial sector has one thing on the office market—it's less cyclical. The big reason the group can sidestep economic dips? Developers can slap up warehouse space quickly, which means that they can respond to fluctuations in the local economy. The long lead time of office building construction—it can take 18 to 24 months to put up a new surburban building—means that developers can find themselves midway through a project just as demand dries up. What's more, unlike office buildings, warehouse facilities need few upgrades over time to keep them competitive.

This very old-fashioned business is being transformed by technology that is rendering older sites inefficient and providing profits for players like ProLogis Trust (PLD).

Hotels

Host Marriott (HMT) and Hospitality Properties Trust (HPT) are the biggest players in this $9 billion business, one of the most cyclical in the REIT universe. The 2001 recession hit the hotel segment extremely hard, pushing income close to zero.

But this isn't the first time the hotel segment has experienced the downside of an economic cycle. Back in the 1980s and early 1990s, hotels were overbuilt and profits eroded. Some markets are smack in the middle of yet another glut of hotel rooms, mainly suburban locations, while some cities have a shortage of rooms.

Clearly, this isn't a sector for risk-averse investors. Because hotel rooms are rented for just a night or two, room rates and occupancy levels can swing dramatically. That works in your favor when the economy is booming, but it's disastrous during an economic contraction. Green Street Advisors' Bracken describes hotels as "businesses masquerading as real estate." Certainly investors in hotel REITs have to have a deep understanding of whether the companies whose stock they buy are solid marketers as well as property managers.

Manufactured Homes

It's not a big piece of the REIT pie, with a market cap of $2.32 billion, but the sector is proving a favorite with investors. Why? Well, first off, forget what you know about the mobile home construction or finance business. Yes, there are a handful of companies that have had terrible results in those businesses, but REITs have found a way to profit from the double-wide. Here's how: REITs own the mobile home communities where owners live. That means they don't have to worry about the low barriers to entry in the mobile home construction business or stay up late wondering whether they've extended too much credit in the subprime market. Instead, they rent the sites that the mobile homes sit on—a steady business in which revenues typically tick up steadily at the rate of inflation or even a little faster. Owners aren't encouraged to move because of the costs of hiring someone to pour a concrete foundation and turn on electric and water services. Chateau Communities (CPJ) is the largest in this sector.

Other small property sectors that merit attention include the self-storage and health care sectors. Self-storage REITs develop and operate self-storage sites. The industry is highly fragmented, which offers opportunities to public companies with access to capital. The bad news? The segment goes through the occasional overbuilding boom and bust.

Health care REITs specialize in buying and leasing hospitals, nursing homes, and medical offices. Since these REITs don't manage their properties, their overhead is very low and balance sheets are fairly stable, says Bay Isle Financial's Block. The downside is that government reimbursement programs can change dramatically with little notice.

Valuing REIT Stocks

Get your hands on any Wall Street research on the REIT industry and you'll be confronted with an array of unfamiliar valuation measures, such as "FFO" and "AFFO." To understand this arcane language, let's first review a bit of accounting. For companies in any business, the goal is to expand profits, right? And most companies are measured by investors on their ability to produce income after taxes, or net income. More net income means higher dividends and better results for REIT investors.

But the way that net income is calculated is that depreciation, the write-off companies get to take to account for wear and tear on their buildings, is treated as an expense. Here's the issue: Most REITs find that their buildings increase in value over time, not dwindle. Land becomes more valuable. Inflation raises rents. And property upgrades boost values. For those reasons, many Wall Street analysts and investors use a measurement called funds from operations (FFO) per share instead of net income per share to measure results for REITs. FFO simply adds back depreciation.

Bay Isle Financial's Block says that FFO can produce an overly rosy view of results, and suggests using adjusted funds from operations (AFFO). This figure refines FFO by recognizing that not all capital improvements enhance property values. Let's say your REIT owns 20 apartment buildings, each of which has a roof with a useful life of 10 years. That means every year the managers would have to replace two roofs. The very act of fixing the roof doesn't mean that rents will rise, though. For that reason, the cost should simply be subtracted from FFO.

Now that you've got the language down and understand the sectors, you're ready to start considering which REITs to invest in.

The Best REITs for Your Portfolio

Once you're ready to put down some cold, hard cash, you could start by trying to ride some of the cycles we've described. But the better strategy, especially for investors who want to buy and hold their stocks instead of trading frenetically, is to pick well-managed companies with strong balance sheets that can weather any storm. Be careful, too, not to pick companies paying the very highest dividends—the most common neophyte REIT investing mistake—because it gives managers little room for error. The last thing you want to do is hold a REIT whose share price falls by half because investors lost confidence after it had to cut the dividend. That's a double whammy.

The better way to invest? Look not only for companies that reward investors with solid dividends, but for those whose shares also appreciate. In other words, you want to find companies that aren't only providing a handsome yield but are also managing their business in such a way that existing properties are throwing off ever-higher rental streams. Also look for a REIT that is expanding its portfolio with new properties over time, which it either acquires or develops on its own.

The list that follows is a starting point for your own research. It's made up of REITs considered steady performers for their sectors. These REITs may not shoot the lights out but they should provide ballast for your portfolio over time and some capital gains to boot.

Equity Office Properties (EOP), the largest REIT by far, has a solid balance sheet and assets. Its founder, Sam Zell, is regarded by many as a visionary in the industry. He's still active in the company's management. The Chicago-based company owns properties sprinkled throughout the country, so you don't have to worry about a regional economic disturbance buffeting Equity Office's performance.

Boston Properties (BXP) is another seasoned operator whose managers are known for slowly accumulating land during downturns so they can be ready when the cycle turns. They own marquee properties, mostly office buildings in four core markets: Boston, San Francisco, Washington, D.C., and New York.

AMB Property Corp. (AMB) invests in industrial properties across the country. Boasting a strong balance sheet, the company invests in big distribution markets located near airports, seaports, and major interstate highways.

Archstone-Smith Trust (ASN) invests in apartment complexes, and with its recent acquisition of Charles E. Smith residential, it also operates high-rise apartment buildings. Unlike some rivals, Archstone-Smith has shown itself to be nimble, selling off assets in markets with less promise and focusing on markets with higher barriers to entry.

Simon Property Group (SPG) is the largest mall operator in the United States and has a proven management team. Its deep relationships with retailers mean that managers can fill vacancies quickly.

If you really want to put your real estate investing on autopilot, consider the **Vanguard REIT Index (VGSIX)**. The fund buys a representative sampling of REIT stocks and holds them, keeping turnover and expenses low. The fund doesn't shoot the lights out, but it has been successful at fulfilling its aim, tracking the Morgan Stanley REIT Index.

Want an actively managed fund? Take a look at **Cohen & Steers Equity Income (CSEIX)**, one of the best-managed of the large-cap REIT equity funds. Marty Cohen runs a well-diversified fund that gives investors exposure in most REIT sectors.

GLOSSARY

adjustable rate mortgage (ARM)
Home loan in which the
interest rate charged varies
over time with the borrower
bearing the risk of rising
interest rates. The initial rate
is set one to four percentage
points below the rate charged
to holders of conventional
fixed-rate mortgages. After an
initial period of one, three,
or five years, the rate resets to
an index such as the prime
rate or a one-year Treasury
bill rate. Depending on the
direction of the index, the
ARM's new rate can float
either up or down. The rate
continues to readjust at regular intervals spelled out in the
contract. Federal guidelines
require that the loans have a
lifetime cap on the total per-
missible adjustment, which is
typically 5 or 6 percent. Also
called variable-rate loans or
adjustable mortgage loans.

annual percentage rate (APR)
The effective rate of interest
for a loan per year. It's different from and higher than the
interest your banker quoted
you on your loan because it
includes the fees.

appraisal   A written estimate
of the fair market value of
the property, typically
conducted by an appraiser.
The value is usually derived
from prices on comparable
properties. Banks use
appraisals to confirm the
value of a property they are
underwriting.

appreciation   Increases in the
value of the property, which
can be caused by inflation,
rising demand, renovation,
and/or expansion. Appreciation gains may be subject to
capital gains taxes when a
property is sold.

basis   For tax purposes, the
cost of a property and the
point from which any depreciation or capital gains will
be computed.

basis point   One 100th of
1 percent.

187

broker's commission   Typically the real estate agent's fee is 6 percent of the purchase price of the house and is split between the seller's and buyer's agents.

buyer's agent   A real estate agent who represents the buyer in a transaction. If the buyer wants to purchase a property listed by that agent's sales office, the real estate agent will typically declare dual agency, representing both seller and buyer. The downside to that arrangement from the buyer's point of view is that the agent may feel beholden to the seller, who is paying the 6 percent commission. Exclusive buyer's agents represent only buyers and are far less common.

capitalization rate   The rate of return of an income-producing property used to calculate a purchase price in the following formula: net operating income (rent minus operating expenses) divided by capitalization rate equals the purchase price. A typical cap rate, though they vary by region, is 10 percent.

cash-out refinance   A popular type of refinancing in which the amount of money received from the new loan exceeds the total of the money needed to repay the existing first mortgage, closing costs, and points. The additional money is typically used to finance renovations or repairs. Such a loan typically comes with a higher interest rate than the usual refinance. Some lenders add a half point to the advertised refinance rate for cash-outs, and many add an additional quarter point if you borrow more than 75 percent of your home's value.

clear title   A title, or proof of ownership, that is free of liens or legal questions as to ownership of the property.

closing costs   Fees paid by both the buyer and the seller at the time property ownership is transferred from one to the other. Typical costs include real estate agents' commissions, discount points, deed recording fees, loan prepayment penalty, appraisal fees, attorney fees, and title insurance premium.

CLUE report   A report from the private Comprehensive Loss Underwriting Exchange that details a home's insurance claim history. It can be useful in determining whether the home you are buying has had a serious history of problems such as water damage. Unfortunately, you won't be able to order one of these reports on your own when you're shopping around for different properties. The best thing to do is to require a CLUE report as a condition of sale.

commercial property As opposed to residential property, commercial property is developed for retail, wholesale, office, apartment, or hotel.

conditional offer Purchase offer made to the seller that is valid only if certain requirements are met by the seller.

condominium A form of property ownership where the owners of individual properties in a development also own interests in common facilities, like elevators, hallways, and recreational areas. For income tax purposes, condominium owners get the same mortgage interest deduction as single-family homeowners.

conforming loan A mortgage loan that is eligible for purchase by Fannie Mae or Freddie Mac, the quasi-governmental agencies that buy mortgage loans from bankers. The maximum loan size is revised each year to reflect changes in the average sales price of single-family homes.

cooperative A form of property ownership in which individuals form a corporation to own an apartment building. The stockholders have a right to use certain apartments and are allowed to deduct interest and property taxes paid by the corporation.

credit report A detailed accounting of a consumer's track record in repaying bills, including mortgages, credit cards, and other loans. Three companies, Equifax (www.equifax.com), Experian (www.experian.com) and TransUnion (www.transunion.com), operate as credit bureaus, supplying lenders with this data. The lenders use this information to decide whether to approve a loan application, as well as the rate of interest to be charged.

credit score A distillation of the credit report frequently used by bankers in determining how much interest to charge a borrower on a mortgage loan. A high credit score means you're more likely to pay your mortgage on time. Scores of 700 and up are considered excellent and are rewarded with the best lending rates. Scoring 600 to 699 is still good, but ranks a B rating, which means you'll pay a little more in interest on your loan. You'll pay at least two percentage points or more over the best rates if your score is 500 to 599. If you score below 499, be prepared to pay three percentage points or more than people with the best credit. The most commonly used score is the FICO score.

curb appeal   The attractiveness of a house or other property when viewed from the street.

deed in lieu of foreclosure   An owner at risk of foreclosure on a property conveys title to the lender to satisfy the debt.

depreciation   For tax purposes, the IRS considers real estate an asset that loses value over time, just as business operators' machinery loses value as it wears down or becomes obsolete. Because of that, owners are allowed to write off a portion of the value of the real estate each year. In the case of residential property, the government puts that useful life at 27.5 years. Commercial buildings like offices or warehouses have a useful life of 39 years. That means, for example, in each and every year you invest in a house you can deduct 1/27.5 of the price you paid, or 3.64 percent, from rental income.

discount points   Money paid to the lender by the seller at the time a loan is originated to account for the difference between the market interest rate and the lower rate of the note.

distressed property   Real estate that is facing foreclosure due to the owners' failure to make mortgage payments.

dual agency   When a real estate agent represents both the buyer and the seller in a transaction, collecting both sides of the commission.

earnest money   The deposit a buyer puts down on a house to show he or she is serious about buying the property.

easement   A right of way giving someone other than the owner access to a property.

encumbrance   Any right or interest in a property that affects its value, such as mortgage loans, unpaid taxes, or easements.

escrow   An agreement between two or more parties that a property or instrument be placed with a third party for safekeeping. For example, earnest money might be placed in escrow prior to the closing of a deal. An escrow agent typically serves this function.

Fannie Mae   A quasi-governmental agency set up to ensure a steady flow of funds in the mortgage market. Fannie Mae purchases mortgage loans from mortgage companies, savings institutions, and commercial banks, which in turn use the proceeds to finance more mortgages. Fannie Mae is the nation's largest investor in residential loans, directly holding or holding in trust one out of every five mortgages in the country. The agency holds some of those mortgages in its own portfolio; in other cases, it issues mortgage-backed securities (MBSs), which it exchanges for pools of mortgages from lenders. The criteria that Fannie Mae and other such agencies set for buying loans set the standard for mortgage guidelines, creating a uniformity in loans that allows them to be combined in pools and sold.

fixed-rate mortgage   A home loan or loan for another sort of a property in which the interest rate remains constant for the life of the loan.

fizbo   Shorthand for the phrase "for sale by owner."

flipping   Strategy by which real estate investors buy a property and quickly resell to others, earning their profit on the flip. The practice became popular during the 1990s, when low interest rates and a burgeoning class of investors interested in developing their own real estate businesses started forming investment clubs around the country. Often they flipped the properties to each other.

foreclosure   A process in which an owner has defaulted on a mortgage and a property is sold.

Typically, the bank itself has to take title to the property, called a REO, or real estate owned. Some investors target this category of real estate because of the potential for finding deep discounts. Lenders typically don't want to hold onto properties.

Freddie Mac Similar to Fannie Mae, Freddie Mac is a public company chartered by Congress to ensure a continual flow of funds to mortgage lenders in support of home ownership and rental housing. Also like Fannie Mae, Freddie Mac packages mortgages into mortgage-backed securities and sells them to investors. Mortgage lenders use the proceeds from selling the loans to Freddie Mac to fund new mortgages.

front foot A standard measurement of land applied at the street line and used for lots of generally uniform depth.

funds from operation (FFO) An alternative measure of profitability used in evaluating real estate investment trusts. The formula is this: net income excluding capital gains or losses from debt restructuring and sales of property, plus depreciation of real property, and after adjustments for unconsolidated entities, such as partnerships and joint ventures, in which the REIT holds interest. The effect is to discount depreciation on real estate. Industry advocates say this is necessary to acknowledge the fact that REITs' primary holding, real estate, actually gains value over time due to appreciation.

gated community A fenced housing community, often with a security guard post at its entry.

general contractor In a renovation, the individual who manages the various tradespeople needed to complete a major project, including carpenters, plumbers, electricians, and others who may themselves freelance as contractors on small jobs.

gross rent multiplier An appraisal method by which the sales price is divided by the monthly rental rate specified in the rental agreement. It allows investors to establish a purchase price when rents and area multipliers are known.

ground lease A lease that rents just the land.

guaranteed replacement cost Homeowner's insurance policy that pays the full cost of replacing or repairing a damaged or destroyed home, even if it is above the policy limit. Over the past 10 years, many insurers have phased out guaranteed replacement policies, after unprecedented catastrophes such as the southern California wildfires and Hurricane Andrew made this kind of coverage too risky to underwrite.

handyman's special A property so in need of repair that its price is discounted.

home equity line of credit (HELOC) Like the name implies, it allows consumers to tap their home equity, but as a line of credit that can be used as needed, like a credit card. A HELOC is backed by that portion of the home that the homeowner owns outright. Interest is generally deductible.

home equity loan A loan based on the amount of equity a homeowner has in the property. The loan is secured by a second mortgage, and is characterized by a fixed rate, payment, and term, usually 5 to 15 years. Interest is generally deductible.

home inspection A detailed examination by a home inspector of readily accessible systems and components of a home. Most inspectors will provide a written report detailing the home's condition. A home inspection is most often paid for by the buyer, and a positive report is often a condition of completion of the sale.

housing expense ratio The formula used by lenders to determine the maximum amount of a borrower's gross monthly income that should be spent on a monthly mortgage payment, including principal, interest, property taxes, and homeowner's insurance. In general, lenders have traditionally limited housing expenses to 28 percent.

income capitalization A term describing the conversion of an anticipated stream of income into a lump sum value. For example, income capitalization would allow a buyer of a multifamily house to convert anticipated rents over the coming year into a fair price for the building. Market value equals the net operating income of a property divided by the capitalization rate.

insurance deductible   The amount you agree to pay before the insurance kicks in. The larger the deductible you take on claims, the lower your premiums, the fees you pay for coverage.

interest rates   The cost of money. There are many types of interest rates that apply to different borrowers. The discount rate is the amount the Federal Reserve charges banks for short-term borrowings. Homebuyers will track mortgage rates, which are based on the yield of 10-year Treasury notes.

jumbo loan   Generally, a mortgage for more than $300,700. Not all lenders offer jumbo loans, and those that do may charge higher rates than they charge on conventional loans.

liability coverage   Home insurance provision that covers compensation arising from claims of injury or damage on your property.

lien   A legal claim on a property that must be satisfied before a property is sold. Typically, a lien will hold a property as security for a debt.

listing agreement   A contract in which a seller hires a real estate agent, usually for 90 days, to market and sell his or her home. The agent hired is usually referred to as the listing agent.

loan commitment   A written proposal to finance a property prepared by a lender and delivered to a borrower. It includes the terms of the loan, meaning the rate of interest and the length of the loan.

loan-to-value (LTV) percentage   The percentage relationship between the principal balance of the mortgage and the appraised value (or sales price if it is lower) of the property. For example, a $100,000 home with an $80,000 mortgage has a LTV percentage of 80 percent.

millage rate   Determined by local governments, the millage rate represents how much property tax you owe per thousand dollars of property value.

mold   Infestations of toxic mold are responsible for raising insurance rates across the country. While mold spores are common and typically pose no problem, they can aggressively collect and grow in damp places, such as a shower stall or wet basement. Exposure to mold inside buildings is detrimental to human health, and can cause everything from hay fever to inflammation of the lungs, asthma, and fungal infections.

mortgage   A loan a homebuyer uses to purchase a house or other property. Under its terms, the buyer gives the lender a lien on the property as security for repayment of the loan. The loan can carry a variety of terms, including fixed or adjustable interest rates, and a 15- or 30-year repayment schedule.

mortgage application   The form a homebuyer fills out to obtain a mortgage. It includes detailed employment and income information on the borrower.

mortgage banker   A person or company that originates mortgage loans, sells them to other investors, and then services the loans, keeping related records and acting as an escrow agent. Most of these loans are insured by a government agency or by private mortgage insurance.

mortgage broker   A person or company that places loans with investors or banks for a fee, but doesn't service those loans.

National Flood Insurance Program   To be covered for flood damage, you have to buy a separate policy from this federally supervised program (800-427-4661).

net operating income   Income from a property after operating expenses have been deducted but before deducting income taxes and mortgage expenses.

"nothing down" investing   A real estate investing strategy in which buyers provide as small a down payment as possible when buying a property. The small down payment magnifies any gain. For example, if a buyer snaps up a $250,000 home with just $5,000 down and the property appreciates 10 percent ($25,000) in the next three years, then that investor's return on the investment is 400 percent. (Were the investor to put down $20,000, the return would be just 25 percent.) A small down payment means, though, that if the value of the property actually declines, you end up paying a mortgage with a value that is higher than the actual value of the property.

operating expenses   What it costs a real estate investor to operate a property. Expenses include maintenance, management, real estate taxes, hazard and liability insurance, utilities, and supplies.

piggyback loan   Loan that bridges the gap between the amount you're able to come up with for a down payment and the 20 percent the bank requires. For example, if you can afford to put down only 10 percent, the mortgage is then structured in two pieces: an 80 percent first mortgage and a 10 percent second mortgage, home equity loan, or home equity line of credit. You avoid paying private mortgage insurance, which is based on the first mortgage. True,

you'll most likely pay a slightly higher interest rate on the second mortgage (one to two percentage points above conventional mortgage rates), but you can always pay it off earlier. A piggyback mortgage can also help you avoid the higher interest rates associated with a jumbo mortgage, if you can keep that first mortgage under $300,700.

PITI   Stands for principal, interest, taxes, and insurance, the four components of a monthly mortgage payment. Principal refers to the part of the monthly payment that actually reduces the mortgage. Interest is the cost of borrowing the money. Taxes and insurance are the amounts paid into an escrow account each month for property taxes, homeowner's insurance, and private mortgage insurance, if any.

point   One percent of the amount of the mortgage loan.

price bubbles   Refers to a situation in which prices for an asset—stocks or housing, for example—rise for an extended period, calling into question whether the assets are overvalued. A bubble in prices raises the specter of a price decline as values return to more normal levels.

private mortgage insurance (PMI)   Lenders require borrowers to put down 20 percent when buying a home. For those who choose or can only afford to put down less, banks require this insurance, which protects the lender in case of default. New financial products, like piggyback loans, allow borrowers to avoid PMI.

property manager   Most resort communities have property management companies that not only act as rental agents but also act as caretakers, sort of surrogate landlords for the homeowners. What's more, a good property management company will know details about the local scene that you might unwittingly overlook. Is there a local lodging tax? What are the rules about on-street parking? Is there a limit to the number of people who will be able to rent your home at one time?

public insurance adjuster   When you face a complicated insurance claim, this professional will do the dirty work of reading the technical jargon and guiding you through the process. They typically are paid a fee of 5 percent of the settlement.

radon   A colorless and odorless radioactive gas found in some homes that can cause health problems given long-term exposure. Home inspectors can test for the existence of unhealthy levels of radon.

rate lock   A commitment from a bank that it agrees to offer a specified rate of interest for a certain period of time.

real estate agent   A person licensed to negotiate and transact the sale of real estate on behalf of the property owner. Realtors are licensed and also hold active membership in a local real estate board that is affiliated with the 800,000-member National Association of Realtors.

real estate investment trust (REIT)   A publicly traded company that owns, and in most cases operates, income-producing real estate such as apartments, shopping centers, offices, hotels, and warehouses. Some REITs also finance real estate. Mortgage REITs make or own loans secured by real estate collateral. A company that qualifies as a REIT is permitted by law to deduct dividends paid to its shareholders from its corporate tax bill. At a minimum, REITs must distribute 90 percent of their taxable income to shareholders. Taxes are paid by shareholders on the dividends received and any capital gains. Losses are not passed on.

real estate owned (REO) Refers to foreclosed properties held by banks. They are typically managed by a third party, who also receives any offers from investors.

retainage The portion of a general contractor's pay, usually 15 percent, that a customer holds back for 30 days after completion of a construction project to make sure everything is working the way it should.

revenue stamps Stamps placed on deeds that show payment of the state's deed transfer tax.

seller carryback An agreement in which an owner of a property provides financing in the sale, often in combination with an assumable mortgage.

soft market Also called a buyer's market, this is a real estate market in which demand for houses has fallen or supply has increased. In such a market, sales prices may stall or even decline.

strip shopping center A commercial development in which each store or business has direct access to a major thoroughfare. Generally without an anchor tenant.

syndication A method by which interest in a property is sold to investors. Typically, a real estate broker, a developer, or anyone else with real estate experience puts together the deal, describing it in a disclosure statement that explains expected returns and the possible pitfalls. The deals can underwrite new construction or an existing property. In either case the investors' stakes typically sell for as little as $10,000 but can go for far more. The syndication can take the form of a partnership, limited partnership, tenancy in common, or corporation.

tax assessment The amount of tax due to a municipality.

title   A document that is evidence of ownership of a property.

title insurance   An insurance policy that protects you if a title or deed is compromised. Typical problems that crop up: Sellers don't own the property; unpaid taxes or other debts are attached as liens to the title, easements restrict use.

total obligation ratio   Also called the debt-to-income ratio, the formula is used by lenders to determine how much total debt an individual theoretically should carry. In general, lenders have traditionally limited overall debt to 36 percent of gross income.

umbrella coverage   Insurance that provides at least $1 million in additional liability protection beyond what you have with your auto and home policies. Umbrella policies cover you and your family in virtually any wrongdoing, from libel and slander accusations to charges stemming from a playground fight.

INDEX